the writer's rules

the writer's rules

The Power of Positive Prose—
How to Create It and Get It Published

helen gurley brown

william morrow and company, inc. ● new york

It is the policy of William Morrow and Company, Inc., and its imprints
and affiliates, recognizing the importance of preserving what has been
written, to print the books we publish on acid-free paper, and we exert our
best efforts to that end.

Library of Congress Cataloging-in-Publication Data
Brown, Helen Gurley.
The writer's rules : the power of positive prose—how to create
it and get it published / by Helen Gurley Brown.—1st ed.
p. cm.
ISBN 0-688-15906-0 (alk. paper)
1. Authorship. I. Title.
PN151.B8   1998
808'.02—dc21   98-22368
                                                        CIP

Printed in the United States of America

First Edition

1 2 3 4 5 6 7 8 9 10

BOOK DESIGN BY DEBBIE GLASSERMAN

www.williammorrow.com

For Guy, Bobbie, Diane, Betty, Myra, Irene, Michael, Mallen, Bonnie D., Barrie, Lisa—intrepid editors who worked with words to make Cosmo *magical*

a c k n o w l e d g m e n t

Deepest thanks to my gifted helper, Myra Appleton, who helped put this book together. Myra was senior text editor at *Cosmo* for twenty years, away for five years to be editor in chief of *Lear's,* then back to *Cosmo* for five years as articles editor.

c o n t e n t s

introduction

Why would I be the one to advise you about writing (I, who didn't even attend college)? Well, I've written seven books and for thirty-two years was editor in chief of the bestselling young women's magazine in the world, *Cosmopolitan*. Why did we do so well? This may surprise some, but I believe that along with other, more obvious elements, it was the writing. Although never singled out for praise or possibly even noticed, the writing in *Cosmopolitan* was singularly effective. Our words created the friendly, big-sister environment that made us the *Cosmo* girl's best friend, adviser and cheerleader, at the same time being clear and literate. The rules for writing for *Cosmo*—and they are stringent, all contained in this book—will help anyone who wants to write better and be published, regardless of the medium, or write letters that will help get the job, the refund, or, help enhance a relationship. *Cosmo*'s intrepid staff, who worked tirelessly on manuscripts, knew what they had to do to make our articles first-rate. During my tenure and under my supervision, seven text editors' principal job, along with assigning, was to *fix* manuscripts, make them sharper and fresher. Why not start with better writing in the first place? What a good idea! Indeed, some of the articles that came in were first-rate on arrival, but not always, not often. After a rewrite (or two or three), the manuscript might be acceptable in terms of research and information, case histories, quotes from respected authorities, sensible conclusions, but the writing itself needed to be made crisper, clearer, more concise, even grammatical! We went to work. If the writer had followed the basic *Cosmo* rules and done what he or she might have, should have, in the first place, we wouldn't have had to do all that fixing. Were our contributors lazy, careless, arrogant? Maybe all or *none* of the above . . . I always thought they were foolish not to turn in work that was a little more professional, but sometimes they were young, sometimes *not* so young, with a certain raw talent but no idea whatever of how to write with discipline, orderliness and style. Editors worked with them as much as they could in phone conversations about needed changes, wrote memos along the same line, but we were not a journalism school. When a manuscript came in about as good as a writer could make it (after many suggestions from the editor), we bought it and went to work, basing *our* work on the rules you'll be reading. Certainly some writers' work didn't need to be fixed and we used them when we could; but all magazines compete for these paragons from a not-large pool, and some publications paid more than we did. Also, throwing big sums at famous writers wouldn't have worked . . . the emotional material we needed wasn't what most of them felt comfortable writing. I preferred that the articles not be by our own staff, though most *Cosmo* editors were published writers. I thought fresh voices from the outside would be more varied and interesting; top contributors might deliver three or four articles a year. Among writers published first or close to first in *Cosmo* were Gail Sheehy, Nora Ephron, Gloria Vanderbilt, Nancy Friday, Veronica Geng, Judith Krantz, Liz Smith and Danielle Steele (poetry).

To tell you a little more about my credentials for advising, that first year at *Cosmo* I did all the editing myself—yes, I was busy! I had no experience as an editor but somehow knew what needed to be done. If the manuscript was boring *me,* despite its acceptable research and content, or was splattered all over the place—splat, splat, splat—I figured it was going to bore and confuse the reader as well. No editing experience whatever, true, but I had loved words for a long time and had had some published at that point. Now perhaps it was time to edit. May I tell you how my love of written words to writing words with nobody paying much attention for years finally led, not only to attention being paid, but to bestselling books and the creation of a magazine? Good! It's hard to stop me, because mine is such a good example of somebody quite ordinary *wanting* to write, *trying* to write, having no particular talent and then "getting there." Some of what worked for me could possibly work for you.

How early can you *be* in love with written words? Early, of course, but for me it wasn't what other people wrote that intrigued me but what I wrote myself . . . baby ego! My sister Mary, four years older than I, was the reader . . . her fines at the Little Rock Public Library were staggering . . . the librarian would let her check out six books at a time before returning the previous six. I read a few little tomes pushed for my age group—*The Bobbsey Twins, Sunbonnet Girls,* later *Nancy Drew* mysteries—but always preferred to *write.* Starting at age six, when I learned penmanship, letters went to family, friends, neighbors, anybody handy; valentines were my specialty. Around age seven I wrote a love letter to eight-year-old Bobby LaCott next door, not reciprocated. A child of the South, at age nine I entered a "What Cotton Means to Me" essay contest. Daddy helped—a tender time between us. The entry didn't win even a handkerchief. Daddy died the next year. The following year— I'm eleven—mother and I went to the World's Fair in Chicago by ourselves, and I wrote to Mary at my grandmother's house in the Ozark Mountains of Osage. "Dear Mary, you ought to see this woman with fans . . . she switches them all around from her front to her back so you can't see anything but the audience makes a big commotion." (Sally Rand *did* cause a big commotion in 1933.) More letters, more valentines, not much reading. At thirteen I actually had a twelve-line poem published in a school "literary" journal, but it was only junior high.

Like most high schools, mine had a thriving newspaper, but I wasn't a contributor, nor was I to the school yearbook, avenues of achievement for *most* serious baby writers. Letters were still my metier. At age fifteen, after my sister contracted polio, I wrote to President Roosevelt. "Dear Mr. President, My sister Mary has been felled by the same thing that you got and I know she'd love to hear from you. Could you write her a letter . . . she's at the Orthopedic Hospital." He wrote: "My dear Mary: Your sister has told me of your illness and I do hope that your stay in the hospital will be very helpful and that you may soon be well on the way to complete recovery. Best wishes to you. Very sincerely yours, Franklin D. Roosevelt." His signature. We checked with a handwriting expert. Franklin's letter hangs in David's and my hallway.

During all those years I still wasn't a book reader but kept a diary as any writer *would.* I thought diaries were pure vanity . . . me, me, me . . . and one day, to show the gods I wasn't as self-centered as they might think, I took a bunch of my diaries out to a vacant lot and burned them up. Mistake! Ridiculous! Not that it will ever be published but keeping a diary is a sensible, practical thing for writers of any age. It not only gets stuff out of your heart and eases the soul but it's *writing,* and the beauty is, you don't have to write carefully or well . . . just enjoy. I type a kind of journal sometimes now that no one will ever see, I don't even go back and read it, but writers *write!* In my twenties I branched out a little from letters and diaries to enter "I Like Ivory soap because" [in twenty-five words or less] contests up the kazoo . . . my investment in Ivory soap wrappers (which had to accompany all entries) ran to about twenty-five dollars, as much as the rent! I had Mary do all the entering from Okmulgee, Oklahoma, where she was in a veterans' hospital trying to learn to walk again (it couldn't happen), thinking Procter & Gamble would feel friendlier toward a girl in a wheelchair in the Midwest than a secretary in an ad agency in Los Angeles. Mary sent the wrappers and entries but refused to send a picture in her wheelchair, although I pleaded . . . it probably wouldn't have helped. No thriller phone calls from P&G, but I did have spanking clean hands (and everything *else*) for a year. Marching along the writer trail, a girl friend who regularly sold scripts to a Saturday morning radio show in Los Angeles for fifty dollars a pop suggested I try. I tried. Nobody bought, no agent clamored to represent me.

What about magazines? Why not? I wrote unasked (you guessed) one article each for *Esquire* and *Glamour*. The rejections were swift . . . at least they responded. I'm twenty-five years old, in my seventeenth secretarial job, having started at eighteen, doing, what else—writing letters. When my boss, Don Belding, chairman of Foote, Cone & Belding, visited his partners in Chicago and New York, I sent three-page state-of-the-office memos to him from Los Angeles—before people made long-distance telephone calls as casually as brushing their teeth. Don's wife, Alice, read the letters and said to her ad-mogul husband, "Don, your secretary writes nicely; why don't you let her try writing advertising copy?" "I need a secretary, not a copywriter," he told her. Life went on. After another four years with Don, I entered *Glamour* magazine's "Ten Girls with Taste" contest. I had the taste of an aardvark but must have filled out a pretty good entry form and was, miraculously, one of the thirteen finalists, flown to New York, put up at the Waldorf and interviewed to become . . . one of the three rejects! Humiliation! Next year I tried again. Out of thirteen thousand entrants, this time—yippee!—I got to be a finalist again and—double yippee!—one of the ten winners. Prize: wardrobe from Joseph Magnin in San Francisco and a trip to Honolulu on the Lurline . . . serious joy! In the entry form, *Glamour* had asked, What do you want to be when you grow up? I knew they didn't want me to say "secretary to Don Belding forever"—though I loved him and my job—so I said "copywriter" . . . Alice had told me about their chat. Soon after my Hawaiian idyll the personnel director at Condé Nast, Mary Campbell, called my boss and said, "Mr. Belding, Helen wants to write copy—why don't you let her?" He did. My first assignment was ten radio commercials for Sunkist oranges. Sound: Telephone rings, receiver up. Grocer's voice: "Hello, the Sunkist navels are in . . . big, juicy, delicious fruit . . . look for the indentation on the side just like a navel . . . blah, blah, blah . . . the ten took two weeks to create, but I was *writing!* Soon the agency put me on the Catalina swimsuit account full-time—writing and getting *paid!* Is that a nice little twenty-five-year odyssey of somebody writing only letters and keeping diaries forever and finally becoming a pro? I think so.

Okay, I'd never had a magazine article published, but along came a book that, not too much later, did lead to editing. Perhaps you've heard the story of my writing *Sex and the Single Girl,* which eventually led to *Cosmo.* I'd left Foote, Cone & Belding and moved to another agency where two other women copywriters and I were getting the same assignments. Though we liked one another, the competition was vicious. One day, walking in Will Rogers State Park, I said to my husband, David, "I'm going to be fired . . . we're all doing the same things . . . can you think of a book I can write . . . you've done that for other people." My brilliant husband said, "Why don't you write about being single? You were like no other single girl I ever knew . . . you were never *home!*" (I was home. The phone was in the fridge so I wouldn't hear it ring—we didn't have answering machines in those days. If I'd heard the phone, I'd have caved in and answered and he'd know I was *not* out, busy and popular. Phone hiding and other techniques I often refer to as trident and castnet (gladiator paraphernalia . . . throw the net over the Christians and gouge them with a fish spear) landed the man. I tried writing the book. I'll tell you in chapter 4 how we found a publisher. Having started by writing letters at age six, with nothing published since except a fifteen-line essay in junior high school and advertising copy, there I am at forty with a bestseller on my hands! Did we expect such a miracle? Of course not. The miracle was getting a book published in the first place, not that it sold well.

Why did it? I told the truth. Reigning philosophy at the time was that if you were female and not married by age thirty, you might as well go to the Grand Canyon and throw yourself in. If you were having sex and not married, don't bother with the Grand Canyon, just go to the kitchen, put your head in the oven and turn on the gas. I knew these ideas were cuckoo. With no research whatsoever except mine and my girl friends', I said you could be a single female and have a fine life; at least, no worse than that of married people, and you didn't have all their problems (mortgages, kids' whooping cough, boundaries set by one man, instead of a world of interesting men to love and learn from), and a single person's sex life was probably better than that of her married friends . . . rejoice, take advantage! The writing was the only kind I knew how to do—simple, direct, succinct— advertising-copywriting training plus friendly, like letters. Suddenly I was getting letters from women all over the country who wanted advice, hundreds of letters weekly, and I was trying to answer . . . type, type, type. One night David looked at me typing and said, "Helen, if you had your own magazine, you could answer everybody at one time!"

We didn't know any better, sat down at the kitchen

table and did up a format, based on ideas from the book plus some other component parts. David took our proposal all over New York. Nobody wanted to start a magazine, but the people at the Hearst Corporation said we could try our format on their once-illustrious but now-hemorrhaging-money *Cosmopolitan*. They gave us a year. Head of New American Library, a publishing company, when our adventure began, David soon returned to Twentieth-Century Fox and left me stranded in my new job, although there was lots of pillow talk and weekend help. Although I was a fledgling editor, *Cosmo* was an immediate success, its first issue selling 900,000 at the newsstand, up from 740,000 the month before, and soon hitting 1,000,000. Writing a book with its subsequent success was pleasurable—*very* pleasurable—but, when I got into it, *editing* suited me like skin. I learned quickly and never looked *up*. As an advertising copywriter, I had absorbed good basics: Get to the point, don't waste words, make your copy sing as well as sell. A double-page ad in *Life* cost $40,000 *then* and the layout provided the copywriter only a four-by-six-inch block for copy and a headline. . . . so the words better be *good*!

During my second year at *Cosmo,* the *Cosmo* editing rules were assembled—twenty-eight of them in sixteen pages, plus eight pages of clichés not to use. Gradually, editors came on staff who specialized in line editing along with other assignments, and the rules were relentlessly followed by these editors and given to every person who wrote for us. Did our writers follow the rules? As I've said, frequently not, but my experience has been that nearly *everybody* needs editing—by someone totally uninvolved with the original writing. Most of our contributors needed this help . . . we gave it guiltlessly. My husband, a longtime magazine editor before he became a movie and theater producer, still looks at my work, edits it when needed, including this book. You won't need that much editing, I solemnly swear, if you follow the rules in this book. Interspersed with the *Cosmo* writer's rules are some thoughts from Strunk and White's *The Elements of Style*, surely the best work ever published on grammar and writing. Every *Cosmo* editor had a copy of *Elements* on his or her desk just as I had as an advertising copywriter. So . . . shall we start making you a first-class writer?

the writer's rules

fifty

rules for

first-class

writing

how do you write "first class"? Very handy for non-hardworking, nondisciplined people to think writers are born, not made . . . the talent is in the genes and just comes out. Hah! Most writers *are* made . . . from desire and need, from endless though not necessarily excruciating hard work—most writers *like* to write. Should you read your brains out . . . other people's estimable work so maybe some of the goodness will rub off? Couldn't hurt, but reading won't make you a writer. I never got through Shakespeare, Tolstoy, e. e. cummings, Jane Austen and a host of other worthies, and reading a book—sorry—never changed my life or helped me become a better writer. As I told you, my avenue was diaries and letters. If reading is your pleasure, *read,* but don't expect the magic to flow from Willa Cather into *you* and the words to come right out of your bone marrow, pre-ordained, and arrange themselves powerfully, perfectly, in sentences and paragraphs. If you want to be a writer, *write.* Write *something.* Write again and again. If nobody sees your output for a while, that's okay; write for *you* until it's time to write for others. House organs and company publications aren't a bad place to start. There's a chapter in this book about how to get a magazine article published—which might be the first thing you sell, and one on selling a book. I'm not going to try to advise on how to create the beautiful words that will inspire, inform and possibly echo through the ages—although others *have* tried to do that in books on how to write. I think your words have to come out of the secret places in you. I see lovely ones all over the place and admire them . . . "the sun scorching down," "cratering economy," "serious cleavage," "big-league restraint," "Hershey-Kisses kisses," "his absence rushing back through me like a train," etc. The monthly *Reader's Digest* feature, "Toward More Picturesque Speech," may inspire you, but you have to do your own writing. Following the rules in this book doesn't necessarily mean you would ever want to write the kinds of books I write or write for a magazine like *Cosmopolitan*. The rules you are going to read (and study?) have only to do with writing nonsloppy, non-slippy-slidy sentences, avoiding the carelessness that annoys editors, and those rules will help you with anything you want to get published. They are all based simply on good common sense.

How do you use them? "The fifty" don't exactly read like a John Grisham novel. On first perusal, the "bad" examples offered may not look all that different to you from the *good* examples, so what's to get so flapped about? Well, the good examples *are* better. Are you supposed to memorize the rules? Gracious, no. I'd suggest, as you begin to write, you simply read them carefully so they get lodged in your consciousness. They surely got lodged in the consciousness of those editors at *Cosmo* all those years and helped them produce clean, clear, interesting, non-waffly, publishable manuscripts. The important thing, of course, as I've said endlessly, is for you to *write* . . . write *something*. Toward having our rules be useful to you, you might want to read them *after* you've written to see if you've been naughty. You can *always* put what you've written through the typewriter or word processor one more time . . . it's nearly always better with that one more try. Of the fifty rules you're next going to see, my favorites (can you have favorites?) are:

4. Stay with the subject. Don't have the reader pounding her head trying to remember what the article is *about*.

7. Vary sentence structure so you don't keep seeing the same pronoun: "She went, she shopped, she dropped, she graduated, she snored" (the *reader* will be snoring).

12. Avoid *it* or *this* or *that* to refer to a situation a few sentences back . . . say this or that *what*.

18. Eliminate a lot of *the*s, *and*s, *as*—just cross them out.

19. Root out *there is* at the beginnings of sentences—cross it out, too, and simply begin. Get rid of a few *what*s and *which*es later on.

The most important rule of all:

43. Death to clichés and tired phrases.

As you write you need to find your own voice, of

course, a way of expressing yourself that will distinguish your style from every other author's. Then, too, will you write fiction or nonfiction. I would love to write fiction but can't. Michael Korda, editor in chief of Simon & Schuster (who has written ten books himself!), cared enough to actually give me a plot for a novel and said, "Now, Helen, go home and write it." Fat chance. (Rats! we'll have to change that . . . *I* have to live without clichés, too. Okay, big chance.) Only wooden, self-conscious sentences came out. If something hasn't actually happened to me or a friend, I can't seem to bring it to life. Novelists are better able to make the switch, possibly to create a memoir or biography. Gore Vidal, Norman Mailer, Joan Didion and Tom Wolfe all write both fiction and nonfiction. Truman Capote mastered both. Dominick Dunne, on the other hand, even turned his own biography *Another City, Not My Own* into a fictional memoir. Find out what you can write; meanwhile these fifty rules couldn't possibly hurt as you are finding *your* voice.

1. Write the way you talk.

Bad: He hied himself down to the emporium to purchase the ingredients of his evening meal before the proprietors ran out of provisions or shuttered for the night.

Better: He hurried to the market to buy what he could for dinner before closing time.

2. Write with clarity. Do *not* opt for the clever turn of phrase if there's even the slimmest chance of its being obscure.

Bad: Sacrifice your soul to beauty and you'll be condemned to be its martyr.

Better: Devote yourself to being beautiful and you're apt to lead an unrewarding life.

3. Don't use the same word (noun, verb, adjective, adverb) more than once in a sentence or paragraph.

Bad: The transportation department issued an edict that taxis could no longer cruise between noon and 3:00 P.M. but must be available at major hotels to provide transportation for people who need taxis to go to the airport.

Better: The transportation department issued an edict that taxis could no longer cruise between noon and 3:00 P.M. but must be available at major hotels for people who need to go to the airport.

4. Stay with the subject of the piece and remind the reader every so often what the subject is. In other words, keep the point of view and focus clearly in mind. That means everything—case histories, the writer's philosophy, statements by authorities—must tie into the theme.

Bad: Erica did change herself, her attitudes, and morals—all in one night—when the notion suddenly came to her that her behavior was inappropriate for the life she wanted. She had been living by a definition of feminine nature that was doing her an injustice. Erica and Forrest were going to get married as soon as he could work his wife around to giving him a divorce.

Better: Erica was determined to change her attitudes and morals once she realized she had been living in a way that could not possibly bring happiness. Yes, she and Forrest were going to be married as soon as he could work his wife around to giving him a divorce, but the working around hadn't happened. By locking herself into a monogamous relationship with a married man, she was more often than not left with no man at all—at least on Christmas Day or even her birthday.

5. A new paragraph with a new thought should flow out of the thought of the preceding paragraph.

Bad: It is common talk that conductors have the biggest egos in music, and perhaps what happened is that Rudel recognized in Keane an ego to match his own and so rewarded it by giving Keane the prestigious job.

Three years ago, Michael Tilson Thomas, now, at twenty-seven, director of the Buffalo Philharmonic, had been assistant conductor of the Boston Symphony Orchestra . . .

Better: . . . Rudel recognized in Keane an ego to match his own and so rewarded it by giving Keane the prestigious job.

Another young conductor who got his big break as suddenly as Keane is Michael Tilson Thomas, now, at twenty-seven, director of the Buffalo Philharmonic. Only three years ago, he had been assistant conductor . . .

6. Don't be profligate with space; run in short paragraphs when possible.

Bad: The hour is noon on a perfect spring day in any big city.

On every street and avenue, new buildings are going up.

Beneath the skeletal girders, construction workers sit, squat and sprawl, munching hero sandwiches, sucking up soda pop, swilling beer.

And ogling what Welsh poet Dylan Thomas called "summery girls," a parade of beauties who are out in force.

They flutter, patter, hurtle and idle from east to west, north to south.

Better: The hour is noon on a perfect spring day in any
big city. On every street and avenue, new buildings are going up. Beneath the skeletal girders,
construction workers sit, squat and sprawl,
munching hero sandwiches, sucking up soda
pop, swilling beer—and ogling what Welsh poet
Dylan Thomas called "summery girls," a parade
of beauties who are out in force . . . fluttering,
pattering, hurtling and idling from east to west,
north to south.

**7. Vary sentence structure to avoid too many
similar noun-verb combos.**

Bad: Mary was twenty-five and so was John. Mary was
Catholic and so was John. They make a congenial and attractive couple; they were relatively
happy together.

Better: Both Mary and John were twenty-five and Catholic. A congenial, attractive couple, they were
relatively happy together.

**8. Break up monster sentences by making two
out of one or using dashes, ellipses, or (more
rarely) a semicolon.**

Bad: Bill spins a record and leans back, resplendent,
glowing with a hip kind of energy, and you find
it hard to believe that this celebrity, number one

Current Check-Outs summary for
Fri Sep 25 15:57:51 PDT 2009

BARCODE: 39048044694705
TITLE: The writer's rules : the power of
DUE DATE: Oct 16 2009

BARCODE: 39048076554744
TITLE: Absolute beginner's guide to Micr
DUE DATE: Oct 16 2009

disc jockey west of Chicago, was, only a month ago, some little bourgeois gnome you wouldn't recognize, just another hardworking grunt in suit and tie who, a year ago, was only one of the 420 deejays in the Los Angeles area, droning on down the years in chorus with the rest of them.

Better: Bill spins a record and leans back, resplendent, glowing with a hip kind of energy. You find it hard to believe that this celebrity, the number one disc jockey west of Chicago, was, only a month ago, some little bourgeois gnome you wouldn't recognize . . . just another hardworking grunt in suit and tie—one of 420 deejays in the L.A. area droning on down the years in concert with his cohorts.

9. Stick to one tense.

Bad: "No," said John. "I can't go to the movies tonight." "Why not?" Sam wants to know.

Better: "No," says John. "I can't go to the movies tonight." "Why not?" Sam wants to know.

10. Position words in a sentence carefully to avoid confusion.

Bad: He lived in a small town that had nothing but a truck-stop café with his mother.

Better: He lived with his mother in a small town that had nothing but a truck-stop café.

11. Place the most important words at the sentence's end.

Bad: Cars that are known as lemons break down as soon as they leave the showroom.

Better: Cars that break down as soon as they leave the showroom are known as lemons.

12. Avoid the use of *it* or *that* or *this* to refer to a situation a few sentences (or even one sentence) back. Preferably say this or that *what* and use a noun in place of *it*.

Bad: All that was too much for Stephanie.

Better: All that criticism was too much for Stephanie.

also

Bad: He took it out to the pier and threw it over.

Better: He took the garbage out to the pier and threw it over.

13. Opt for the straightforward statement rather than the convoluted, no matter how stylish the latter may seem.

Bad: Open marriage, group marriage, communes: the intricate network of the new connections pioneers of the seventies are forging to expand human closeness on the far side of traditional family structures.

Better: Open marriage, group marriage, communes—all are alternatives to the traditional family . . . experimental lifestyles that the disenchanted are turning to in their search for more intimate communication.

14. Use the active voice, not the passive.

Bad: Learning a new language is often difficult for me.
Better: I often have difficulty learning a new language.

15. Be specific rather than general.

Bad: She liked pretty, feminine things.
Better: She liked Wedgwood, chintz and ruffles.

16. Phrase statements positively, not negatively.

Bad: She did not like chocolate ice cream as much as she liked vanilla.
Better: She preferred vanilla ice cream to chocolate.

17. Do not use shorthand. Save acronyms for the chronologically oriented and for second mentions.

Bad: You can often make more of a profit buying OTC than on the AmEx—and OTC stocks are generally cheaper.
Better: You can often make more of a profit by buying over the counter (OTC) than on the American

Exchange—and OTC stocks are generally cheaper.

18. Eliminate the unnecessary pronouns, conjunctions and articles (*you, he, and, the, a,* etc.) from sentences.

Bad: Eloise had the responsibility of picking up the children (six-year-old Alvin and the toddlers), the station wagon from the garage, and getting supplies for the whole weekend into the car and driving to Connecticut.

Better: Eloise's responsibilities included picking up the children (six-year-old Alvin and his toddler siblings), getting her station-wagon from the garage, buying supplies for a whole weekend, then driving everything and everyone to Connecticut. (Notice we got rid of five *the*s!)

19. Leave out superfluous words, particularly *There is* at the beginning of a sentence and *that* later on.

Bad: There is a kind of anxiety that is free-floating, a general feeling of apprehension that is not attached to any specific type of anxiety.

Better: Free-floating anxiety is characterized by a general feeling of apprehension not attached to any specific activity.

also

Bad: Due to the fact that he was broke, he had to walk the three miles to his studio every day.

Better: He was so broke he had to walk the three miles to his studio every day.

or

Being stone broke, he had to walk the three miles to his studio every day.

20. Stay away from vague adjectives that do nothing but clutter a sentence.

Bad: She has a little bit of a temper, especially when she's feeling really tired.

Better: She has a bit of a temper, especially when she's feeling tired.

Better yet: She has a temper, especially when she's tired.

21. Let adjectives be adjectives. Do not tart them up into adverbs by adding *ly*.

Bad: She carried on a conversation with herself pixilatedly.

Better: She carried on a conversation with herself, as if she were pixilated.

22. Stay away from the *moreover* school of writng—that is, avoid excessive use of words and phrases such as *moreover, furthermore, for instance, for example* and *incidentally.* Such adverbs and adverbial phrases can almost always be omitted.

Bad: Everyone I know seems to be into touch therapy.
         Nell, for example, is. So is Sarah, incidentally.
         Moreover, so am I.
Better: Everyone I know seems to be into touch therapy.
         Nell is. Sarah is. So am I.

or

         Everyone I know seems to be into touch therapy.
         Nell, Sarah and I are all involved.

23. Use a colon to add impact and eliminate unnecessary words and phrases.

Bad: She had a problem, which was how she should cope with the situation.
Better: Problem: how to cope with the situation.
         (Notice we eliminated a *which was, which* and *that* often being unnecessary in a sentence.)

also

Bad: The result was that she was left in despair.
Better: Result: She was left in despair.

24. Let nouns and verbs, not their modifier, carry the weight of a sentence.

Bad: She felt her heart soar elatedly with all its might.
Better: Elated, she felt her heart soar.

25. Do not hesitate to split an infinitive.

Bad: Genuinely to forgive can sometimes take forever.
Better: To genuinely forgive can sometimes take forever.

26. Do not hesitate to end a sentence with a preposition.

Bad: A preposition is something with which I would not end a sentence.
Better: A preposition is something I would not hesitate to end a sentence with.

27. Unless you are a recognized authority on a subject, profound statements must be attributed to somebody appropriate.

Bad: All psychiatrists are basically Freudians.
Better: According to one practitioner who specializes in group therapy, "All psychiatrists are basically Freudians."

28. Identify people immediately—not even one sentence later—and identify them completely.

Bad: As Dr. Malcolm Reis points out . . .
Better: As Dr. Malcolm Reis, director of obstetrics at New York's Mount Sinai Hospital, points out . . .

or

As pointed out by Dr. Malcolm Reis, director of obstetrics at New York's Mount Sinai Hospital . . .

29. If several pages have elapsed between the introduction of a person and the next mention of him or her or between the occurrence of an incident and a later reference to it, identify the individual or situation again briefly.

Original: Arthur Jones, Ph.D., professor of English at the University of Toronto, who specializes in Restoration drama . . .

Later ref: Dr. Jones, the Restoration drama professor from Toronto . . . (Not merely "Dr. Jones.")

also

Original: With her bank account empty, Sarah went to her uncle to beg a loan to pay the rent.

Later ref: That loan Sarah secured from her uncle helped balance . . . (Not merely "That loan helped balance. . . .")

30. When mentioning a well-known person, give the name first, then follow with his or her credentials.

Bad: One of the three remaining duchesses of Palm Beach society is Ms. Ogilvy Smathers, who often entertains lavishly.

Better: Ms. Ogilvy Smathers, one of the three remaining duchesses of Palm Beach society, often entertains lavishly.

31. When writing about a person who is not a celebrity, give her or his identity first, followed by the name.

Bad: Mary Garson, twenty-seven years old, the daughter of a psychiatrist, has been in analysis for three years.

Better: Twenty-seven years old, the daughter of a psychiatrist, Mary Garson has been in analysis for three years.

32. Don't go into ancient biographical detail about civilians—i.e., keep high school achievements, hometown experiences, childhood traumas to a minimum and concentrate on the area of their lives that prompted you to write about them in the first place. Even with celebrities, early-life details are usually less interesting than more recent facts.

33. When quoting someone, use the simple *said* rather than *stated, exclaimed, cried, yelled, shouted, groaned, smiled, frowned* (nobody ever smiles or frowns a sentence). If you want to convey the emotion with which a statement was spoken, add a few words of explanation.

Bad: "Don't touch me," she teased.
Better: "Don't touch me," she said, the smile on her lips
        as playful as the lilt in her voice.

34. Do not clutter the attribution of quotes with so-called descriptive adverbs.

Bad: "I loathe you," she said furiously.
Better: "I loathe you," she said, her voice rising in fury.

35. When quoting people, have them speak informally, as they would in conversation (with contractions, etc.), not as they would in formal writing.

Bad: "He is just divine. He is somebody I enjoy being
        with . . . enjoy talking to. We rap about his cur-
        rent girl, or about Paul, and it is so much fun. If
        he were not my cousin, though, I do not know if
        we would have fallen into this intimately friendly
        pattern so easily—we would probably have had
        to get the mating game out of the way first."
Better: "He's just divine. I really enjoy being with him,
        talking to him. We rap about his current girl, or
        Paul, and we have a lot of fun. If he weren't my
        cousin, though, I don't know if we'd have fallen

into this intimately friendly pattern so easily—
we'd probably have had to get the mating game
out of the way first."

36. Do not use dialect unless you are a native.

Bad: "I wooda gone home but I couldna find my way."

Better: "I would've gone home but I couldn't find my way."

37. If you have a brief quote followed by several sentences about the person, sometimes you can subsume those sentences into the quote itself to make it stronger.

Bad: Adrienne admits to having gotten the job "because I knew the president of the company." But her connections didn't make the work any easier. She did every kind of menial chore—ran errands, typed speeches, clipped newspapers. And she was paid only the minimum wage: "A dollar-forty an hour . . . something like that."

Better: Adrienne admits to having gotten the job "because I knew the president of the company. But my connections didn't make the work any easier. I did every kind of menial chore—ran errands, typed speeches, clipped newspapers. And I was paid only the minimum wage—a dollar-forty an hour . . . or something like that."

38. When writing dialogue, be sure to periodically remind readers who is speaking which lines.

39. Make sure antecedents are clear.

Bad: The image of Microsoft's Bill Gates loomed large over Apple's acting leader, Steven Jobs, as he announced their alliance.

Better: The image of Microsoft's Bill Gates loomed large over Apple's Steven Jobs as the latter announced their alliance.

40. Keep similes and metaphors to a minimum—and don't mix the latter.

Awful: He was drowning in debt at such a rapid clip that the sands of time threatened to run out.

41. Keep so-called dirty words, even in this age of frankness, to a minimum. Also avoid the vernacular in describing sexual activities or organs.

Bad: Screwed, fucked, laid, balled, came, etc.
Better: Made love, had intercourse, reached orgasm, climaxed.

42. Update your language: Avoid passé words and dated slang, such as *groovy, swinging, all that jazz, freaked out, zonked, you'd better believe it.*

43. Root out all clichés and even words that are just slightly tired. (See chapter 2.)

44. Don't use *hopefully* to mean anything but *in a hopeful manner*.

Bad: Hopefully, Joan will get the job she has been after for two years.

Better: We're all hoping Joan gets the job she has been after for two years.

or

Joan's been after the job for two years; we hope she gets it!

45. Learn the difference between *which* (to introduce part of a sentence that's *not* essential—the word always preceded by a comma) and that (to introduce part of a sentence that *is* essential), and use the words appropriately.

Bad: This is the house which Jack built.

Better: This is the house that Jack built.

also

Bad: German is a difficult language that comes as no surprise to anyone who's tried to master it.

Better: German is a difficult language, which comes as no surprise to anyone who's tried to master it.

46. Learn the difference between *who* (people) and *that* (nearly everything else), and use the words appropriately.

Bad: He had friends that were unusually supportive.
Better: He had friends who were unusually supportive.

47. Although gadfly grammarians have been predicting the demise of *whom* for decades, the careful writer will know how *whom* differs from *who* (of which *whom* is the objective case) and use the two appropriately.

Bad: Who did you give the pages to?
Better: To whom did you give the pages?
        (You wouldn't *begin* to say "Never ask to know for who the bell tolls," would you?)

48. Don't be relentlessly depressing. Even if the subject you are writing about is downbeat (as in women in prison), search out the positive efforts being made to improve the situation. At the same time, do not depart from the truth for the sake of telling a good story.

49. Never rewrite or edit just for the sake of change, only for improvement.

50. And, of course, never borrow from other writers without acknowledging the debt. Let me do that now: Many of the rules in this chapter can be found, stated differently, in that elegant bible of good writing, *The Elements of Style,* by William Strunk, Jr. and E. B. White.

Okay, you've been told all about bad phrasing . . . don't do this, don't do that. What about writing beautifully . . . finding the nouns, verbs, adjectives that will glow and sparkle, excite, enchant and inspire your readers? You're absolutely on your own! I know you've got them in you . . . *you're* going to get them out!

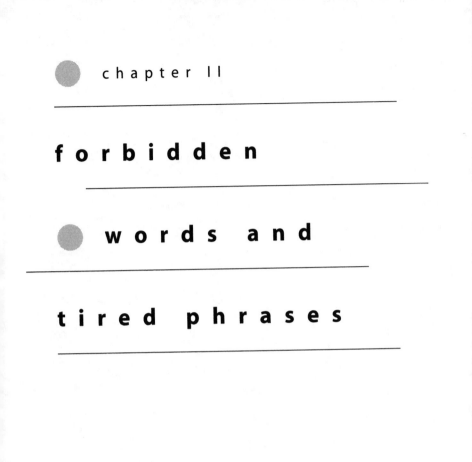

chapter II

forbidden

words and

tired phrases

Clichés are phrases so familiar that we often use them in writing and speaking to avoid the trouble of thinking of something more original. A convenience, yes, a kind of shorthand, but so very trite, stale and lazy. Don't know whether I used clichés before I became an editor and started to realize how deadly they are. Probably not in my writing—you had to be fresh and foxy in advertising—but I probably did when I talked to people ("blue is your color," "let's take a breather," "a lot of flap over nothing," "have a nice day," etc.). Now I try not to use too-familiar phrases even in talking or favorite words over and over. Sometimes I get a crush on words and they crop up endlessly, and I now try to stay away from those too. I've just called a moratorium on *indigenous, component parts, juxtaposition, primordial*—five darling words I "discovered," love, used excessively and am trying to live without for a while. Maybe it's a little nutty or pretentious not to want to even *say* the same things in a tired way—but not bad discipline. I wasn't really aware of clichés until I got to *Cosmo*, but, as the manuscripts came in and clichés would stick out like—no; not sore thumbs . . . like pimples? blue eyeshadow?—I thought and continued to think through the years, "These *silly* people . . . writing so tired, so predictable, so sloppy." *Cosmo* editors ruthlessly, guiltlessly eliminated clichés. How many can *you* spot in the following paragraph?

Mary is known for giving as good as she gets. When Steve, trying to get her goat, told her she was ugly as sin, she was all over him like a tent. Who did he think *he* was, God's gift to women? Not on your life, thought Mary. She could spot a sitting duck when she saw one, and in this case, Steve stuck out like a sore thumb. She went after him tooth and nail, calling him every name in the book, until he finally cried uncle and slunk away with his tail between his legs, a sadder but wiser man who learned his lesson the hard way.

Give yourself a perfect score if you came up with fifteen clichés packed into those 109 words—with not an original thought among them. To further test your Cliché Quotient, here is a beginner's list of tired and tiresome phrases I hope you'll never want to use, at least not in your writing. Can you live without them . . . *all* of them?! Yes, you can, and you'll find your writing and speaking much fresher and livelier for the effort.

Animals: Furred, Finned, Feathered and Four-Footed

Fish or cut bait

Big fish in a small pond

Fish out of water
Better fish to fry
Smells fishy
Happy as a clam
At a snail's pace
Wolf down your food
Free as a bird
Eat like a horse/bird
Kill two birds with one stone
For the birds
Eat crow
Eagle eye
The early bird catches the worm
Bird's-eye view
A bird in the hand is worth two in the bush
As the crow flies
Wild-goose chase
Ugly duckling
Kill the goose that lays the golden egg
Talk turkey
Lame duck
Duck soup
Sitting duck
Proud as a peacock
Crazy as a loon
Don't count your chickens before they're hatched
Don't put all your eggs in one basket
Chicken out

A dog-eat-dog world
Top dog
Let sleeping dogs lie
Gone to the dogs
Sick as a dog
Dirty dog
Dog days
Hair of the dog
Dog tired
Hounds of hell
Fight like cats and dogs
Rained cats and dogs
Pick of the litter
A dog's life
Cat's meow/pajamas
Fat cat
Let the cat out of the bag
Like a tiger in bed
Have a tiger by the tail
Lion's share
Eager beaver
Bug off
Knee-high to a grasshopper
A fly in the ointment
Butterflies in your stomach
Cart before the horse
Dark horse
Don't look a gift horse in the mouth

From the horse's mouth
Hold your horses
Bull in a china shop
Take the bull by the horns
Shoot the bull
Sacred cow
Gets my goat
Black sheep
Quick like a bunny
Sly as a fox
Dumb like a fox
Pig out
Go whole hog
Cast pearls before swine
Fat as a pig
Male chauvinist pig
In a pig's eye
Crocodile tears
White elephant
Memory like an elephant's
Blind as a bat
Like a bat out of hell
Bats in the belfry
Smell a rat

Body Parts and Fluids
Doesn't have the stomach for it
Make no bones about it

Bared her soul
Not just another pretty face
Let's face it
In your face
A nose for news
Cut off your nose to spite your face
It's no skin off my nose
Keep your nose clean/to the grindstone
Talk your ear off
Rule of thumb
Rocks in his head
Let it slip through the fingers
Lend an ear
Ear to the ground
Let me bend your ear
I'm all ears
No grass growing under his feet
Read my lips
Easy on the eyes
See eye to eye
In the blink of an eye
Reduced to tears
A shoulder to cry on
Give the cold shoulder
Head and shoulders above
A chip on his shoulder
Bosom buddies
Biting the hand that feeds you

Go hat in hand
Win hands down
At his fingertips
Cut to the quick
Achilles' heel
Head over heels in love
Kicked up his heels
Down at the heels
Have a leg up
On his last legs
Put your best foot forward
Footloose and fancy free
Putting your foot in your mouth
On the tip of her tongue
Down in the mouth
My heart was in my mouth
Wearing your heart on your sleeve
My heart wasn't in it
Bum ticker
Shove it down your throat
Put your money where your mouth is

Money and Other Specie

Two sides of the coin
Not worth a plugged nickel
A dime a dozen
Nickeled and dimed to death

Turn/spin on a dime
Put my two cents in
Sound as a dollar
Phony as a three-dollar bill
Bet your bottom dollar

Mealtime and Other Comestibles

Out to lunch
That's the way the cookie crumbles
Cool as a cucumber
Couch potato
Top banana
Second banana
The whole enchilada
The apple of his eye
Goodies
Yummy
Eat my words
Don't mince words
Against the grain
Stuffed to the gills
Get on the gravy train
Life is just a bowl of cherries

Truth and Other Colors

Moment/kernel of truth
Truth to tell

If truth be told
Tried and true
True to form
Revealing your true colors
Passed with flying colors
Once in a blue moon
Out of the blue
Talk a blue streak
Green with envy
Green-eyed monster
Green around the gills

Geography
Far-flung places
Far and wide
Four corners of the world/globe
It's a small world
All over the map
The Big Apple (for NYC)
La La Land (for L.A.)
Lotus Land (for L.A.)
Tinseltown (for L.A.)
The Windy City (for Chicago)

The Elements
Throw caution to the wind
Right as rain

Tip of the iceberg
Cold as ice
Skating on thin ice
Ice maiden/princess
Pure as the driven snow
Go with the flow

Life and Death

Alive and well and living in . . .
Chance of a lifetime
Scared to death
Give up the ghost
Bites the dust

Perfection . . . or Nearly So

To a fare-thee-well
To a tee
To the manner born
Put on the ritz
Dressed to kill
Dressed to the nines

The Nether World

All hell broke loose
A snowball's chance in hell
Come hell or high water
Gone to hell in a handbasket
When hell freezes over

Ageism
Woman of a certain age
Long in the tooth
Younger than springtime
May–December/September romance

Love and Marriage
Connubial bliss
A marriage made in heaven
Mabel married the man of her dreams/Mr. Right/Mr.
  Wonderful
Prince Charming
Knight in shining armor

Weaponry and Ammo
She went ballistic
A shot in the dark
Bite the bullet
Crack the whip
Smart as a whip
Come on like gangbusters
Lick his wounds
Armed to the teeth

Push Me, Pull Me and Other Movements
Pull out all the stops
Pull no punches
Roll with the punches

Roll over in his grave
When push comes to shove
Jumped at the chance
Jump the gun
A leap of faith
Time flies
Fly off the handle
Flies right out the window
Hit the roof/road
Walk a tightrope/fine line
Run the gamut (from A to B)
Running on empty
Trip the light fantastic
Cut to the chase
Kicked over the traces
Alive and kicking
Throw/toss in the towel
Throw the baby out with the bath water

The Sporting Life

Go to bat for
Get the ball rolling
A whole new ballgame

New Age

First, the good news:
Different strokes
Brain-dead

Space cadet
When the going gets tough
Do the math
There is no there there
Talk the talk and walk the walk
It's déjà vu all over again
It ain't over till it's over
You don't have to be a rocket scientist/brain surgeon
Pushing the envelope
Bummer
Been there, done that

A Potpourri of the Miscellaneous

John loves hamburgers. He *is not* alone.
Experts agree
The path of least resistance
A little bell went off
Lit up like a Christmas tree
Sadder but wiser
One girl's story
A come-hither look
A perfect 10
Battle of the sexes
Catch as catch can
Old-boy network
It's old hat
Go figure!
It's for the best

Best of both worlds
Here today, gone tomorrow
If it's not one thing, it's another
No strings attached
Go down the tubes
Gone but not forgotten
Off the deep end/beaten track/wall
Skim/scratch the surface
Six of one, half a dozen of the other
Not worth the paper it's written/printed on
When the chips are down
High-wire act
High as a kite
Thin/skinny as a rail
Run it up the flagpole
Leave no stone unturned
A far cry from
Chances are
Knock on wood
Don't knock it
Control freak
To the nth degree
Knows no limits/bounds
Quick on the draw
Hit me like a ton of bricks
Ulterior motive
No-nonsense
It stands to reason
Against all odds

Going for broke
Whopping raise
The bottom line
The rest is history
Ugly as sin
Nitty-gritty
Between you and me and the gatepost/lamppost
Font of information/wisdom
Everything but the kitchen sink
In the pipeline
Window of opportunity
Photo op
Hard as nails
Left a lot to be desired
Fraught with danger/peril
Coming up roses
Beat around the bush
Traipsing
Heard through the grapevine
And last but not least . . .

As for *forbidden* words, remember:

1. A *male* is a man or boy.
   A *guy* is a rope, chain, rod or wire.
2. A female is a woman or a girl.
   A *gal* is a unit of acceleration or the abbreviation for gallon.
3. Do not use *for example, for instance.*

Substitute *say, take, perhaps.*

4. Do not use *in fact.*

   Substitute *indeed, in truth.*

5. Do not use *looking to make a change.*

   You look to a noun, not a verb.

6. When using *wise* as a suffix, confine it to legitimate words, as in *clockwise* and *sidewise.* Refrain from cobbling it to words it was never meant to complete, as in *jobwise* or *mathwise.*

Okay, you'll never be a cliché addict again . . . good!

chapter III

how to get

a magazine

article

published

i never had a magazine article published until a couple of years ago. One afternoon I just decided to do up a little piece—they didn't ask, I didn't query—for *Fortune* magazine. The idea: *Cosmo* was the most successful young woman's magazine in the world (brag, brag), and success came from having the best people working for me. Nobody ever left; top editors stayed fifteen, twenty-five, thirty years, whereas at some magazines and other companies the revolving doors never quit spinning—expensive, disruptive. As a boss, I must have been doing something right, right? To keep good players anchored and, ergo, product selling, I suggested Get lots of input from them, and then *you* decide. . . . hand down a plan. Be very clear about what you want, and don't waffle later. Get back to people who need decisions quickly. Go to *their* offices . . . takes less time than if they came to yours; remember their personal life is as important as their office life (surprise, surprise!); you'd better kick in with help; don't criticize anybody in front of anybody else; give all the credit away, blah, blah, blah. Cute article. I sent it to the editor in chief of *Fortune,* who I didn't know, but he accepted it without changes. This experience probably won't have a great deal to do with *your* magazine-writing tries which will surely kick in sooner, except that I followed my own rules for clear, lively writing and they worked!

At *Cosmo* we had forty-six to forty-eight different features in every issue, so we needed a lot of stuff—and not written by our staff, as I mentioned. Occasionally we pulled something out of what is called the "slush" (unsolicited manuscripts) and bought it. Assistants were trained to do a first read and, if they liked a piece, could pass it along to their bosses, but you can't depend on a slush search at very many magazines. Through the slush or otherwise, many neophyte writers with promise came into *Cosmo*'s and my life through the years and got published, which is why I feel qualified to tell you how it can happen—to *you*. *Some* promising people made it, some didn't. Our managing editor, Guy Flatley, always said you couldn't denigrate what anybody learned in college or from *writing* in college. The more writing the better, although poetry classes were sometimes the sole writing experience of his would-be assignees; he said raw talent could be sensed, however. Senior editor Diane Baroni remembers a young lady working in a pizza parlor in Coraopolis, Pennsylvania, whose manuscript was pulled from the slush because it had *"something."* Through the years Diane worked with her pizza-parlor find, who got better and better all the way to major. There was one young discovery who'd had more romantic experiences overseas (or said she'd had them) than a traveling rock star and chronicled them all for us. "I was crazed for a Venetian boatman—we made it in his gondola," "The night a Saudi prince gave me a ruby pendant, no strings attached" (we didn't demand that the writer produce the pendant), "Bicycling through the Ruhr Valley with Rolf was just the beginning," etc. We never knew how this writer had time to *write,* but she got it all down. Another raw talent gofered for a stand-up comic, and his every sentence had to be translated into English—no sense whatever of style, grammar, transitions, logic or progressions, but Diane brought him along. Guy said *some* writers, rather than being too structureless, came to him straight from an English literature course and had been subjected to almost too *many* rules. . . . they had to be loosened up, rescued from flowery. If someone unknown sent a well-written letter along with a few samples of his or her work, even from nonimpressive publications (small-circulation newspaper, shopping news), asking for *any* kind of assignment, we let that person come in and "go through the books"—two big loose-leaf binders, one containing ideas for emotional articles, the other for nonemotional ones. The writers could study the books, choose one or two ideas to try, photocopy the pages, take them home and go to work. Some neophyte writers got to write regularly for us that way. Even our top writers sometimes went through the idea books.

How much will a magazine's staff help you with an

assigned article that looks promising on arrival but needs more work before they buy? Some, lots or none, depending on the magazine. Our system: Over the phone, the assigning editor would go over with the writer what was needed in his turned-in manuscript, all the way from a page-by-page discussion that could take twenty minutes to a less detailed, more general analysis. Editor might *write* a critique of what was needed, send manuscript back with the requested changes, too-stuffy or too-flowery patches, clichés and tired phrases circled. Usually we didn't go over manuscripts with the writer in the office. Office visits tend to escalate into personal chats, and nobody has time for open house. For those articles worth buying but still needing lots of work after even possibly a third rewrite—we bought. *Cosmo* editors then went to work—edited, retyped, edited and retyped in several progressions. Paragon editors themselves may not get it perfect with the first edit because there is no *end* to the work that can be done to improve a manuscript; at the same time, you don't want to flatten it out or get rid of any sparkle. Many of the writers we discovered got better and better and gradually needed *less* fixing and organizing. Others never did "get it" in terms of good, clear, smooth writing but were good reporters, so we bought their articles and fixed them ourselves.

Listen, what happened at "my magazine" is not necessarily typical of any other nor can I promise that you'll be "discovered," but if you write carefully, try to absorb the fifty rules for good writing in chapter 1, eliminate clichés and tired phrases in chapter 2, query professionally, I think you've got a shot. Maybe you won't even be one of the heavily fixed ones! My own conviction is that selling a magazine article isn't *that* difficult. More than ten thousand magazines (Magazine Publishers Association figures) were published in the United States in February 1998, and nine hundred new ones were started, many of which, old and new, buy freelance material. For the most part, magazines don't *pay* all that scrumptiously for all that work, but remember we need *you* more than you need *us*! Okay, let's start with the seven basics that can help you get published. You have an article idea?

1. Research the market.

Find the magazine or magazines that might be interested in your idea. It is totally dumb to send a query or completed manuscript to a publication that couldn't possibly care. If you have in mind writing a piece on the mating habits of lions, say, you wouldn't pitch the idea to *Popular Mechanics* or *Vogue,* but, along with publications that deal specifically with wildlife, you might think of *Cosmo* because the magazine is animal-friendly. You know *that* from having studied several issues. Do study as many magazines as you can—really get the feel of them—in order to become familiar with their format and the range of subjects they cover.

2. Send a query letter.

This is the letter intended to sell your idea. Address it to the articles or features editor, or department head listed on the masthead if your idea fits neatly into that person's category (health, beauty, lifestyle, etc.). Magazines are all structured differently, and some managing, deputy or executive editors actually read raw material—but not many. So, you're better off *not* submitting anything to the top editor unless he knows you. Even then, upon receiving your article or query, this person will probably pass it along, unread, to one of his editors, who will evaluate the piece and send it back with an opinion to the chief, who will make the final decision. Sometimes, an opinion is asked for from more than one person. An editor in chief trusts his subordinates' judgment and recommendations or they wouldn't be there, so you're safe entrusting your precious manuscript to somebody other than the head raccoon.

At *Cosmo* the assigning editor got the article in. If promising enough, it went on to the managing editor (the boss under me), then on to me—by this point the piece might have already gone through two or three rewrites by the writer. If there was a disagreement—assigning editor liked it, managing editor didn't—I might even send it along for a third editor's opinion. I didn't often study my brains out to see whether the yea or nay vote should be supported but went with the majority—two for, one against, we bought; two against, one for, we didn't. With reason, I trusted my evaluators totally.

• Plan ahead. Keep in mind that magazines have what is called a lead time, and it's long. You wouldn't propose a Valentine's Day article any later than September or October, or a Christmas article later than July, for monthly magazines.

• Keep the query short and to the point, and make it as well crafted as your article will be. Try for a "wow" title, then explain what will be in the piece, why you think the subject important or timely. Don't say your idea is just right for the magazine you're querying; the recipient doesn't need to be told what subjects are appropriate for the publication he or she lives with daily.

• You might say a few words about your special qualifications for writing the article—personal experience, researched the subject for a long time, etc.—but don't be boring! Explain the manner in which you intend to cover the material: running narration, first person, Q&A, bulleted or numbered points. Include the number of words you intend to write, length of time you will need to complete the piece and authorities you plan to consult.

• Mention your writing credits and include clips. If you haven't any—i.e., you've never been published—offer to write on spec. This means you will complete the article and submit it with no guaranteed payment, the standard procedure for someone who is just getting started, particularly if you want desperately to write for a particular publication. Established writers get a kill fee if an article is rejected; novices usually don't.

- Don't promise more than you can deliver, either in length or content. No good suggesting a 10,000-word article to a magazine whose longest piece runs 2,000 words (you've already heard about researching the publication before you query). Make sure your idea is length-appropriate.

Here is a good query.

TITLE: On-the-Job Romance: How to Do It Right
LENGTH: 2,000 words
DELIVERY: One month from date of assignment
WRITER: Miranda Crain (see attached clips)

Gist of Article:

If you got a raise every time someone said, "Don't become involved with anyone at work," you'd be richer than the CEO of your company. But in truth, sometimes you *do* fall for someone at the office. (Here, I'll give the stats on the number of couples in this country who indeed do meet, mate, marry on the job.) After all, you spend eight hours a day there. And the fact that a funny, cute, sexy man is a co-worker doesn't make him any less funny, cute, or sexy, which means you'd be crazy to write off work as a place for cultivating romance. But you have to cultivate it right. This piece will go beyond the clichéd warning "Don't mix business with pleasure" to give solid advice on how to navigate a very real and often gummy situation that you may one day be lucky enough to find yourself in. Organized around twelve office-romance rules, it will be a lively blend of commentary from corporate and industrial psychologists who specialize in the human element of the workplace, advice from personnel directors who make and enforce the rules—but what do they really think about office romance?—and especially anecdotes from women who have managed an office romance with panache, some of whom have seen the liaison through to marriage. Here, briefly, are the rules that I'll flesh out:

1. Don't jump into the romance. This means never start it drunk. And always wait a while before sleeping with him.

2. Don't advertise. You don't know who among your colleagues might hold the romance against you.

3. At the same time, don't act like you're not friends.

4. Present a unified front. What good does your discretion do, after all, if he's letting co-workers in on the secret?

5. If word nonetheless leaks out and a colleague asks you about the affair, be evasive and noncommittal until you're ready to go public.

6. If the romance happens to stick and you don't mind people in the office knowing, let them figure it out for themselves anyway. Don't babble.

7. If the romance takes off, try not to work on projects together.

8. Don't let the affair change the way you talk in meetings—either about him or to him.

9. Never, ever give into the temptation to have sex in the office, no matter how strong the urge.

10. Don't discuss your salaries—at least not at the beginning.

11. If the affair turns out to have been a mistake, you'll want to tell him nicely that it was fun, it's over, and you'd appreciate its remaining private.

12. Whether the romance works out or not, don't quit over it. He wouldn't, and your job isn't any more dispensable than his.

I'll also include a brief sidebar titled "Do You Dare to Date the Boss?" with anecdotal quotes from women who've done so and how they fared.

I would, of course, welcome any suggestions you may care to make. Meanwhile, I eagerly await your response.

This, too, is a good query, but of another sort:

TITLE: What's Your Genetic Prognosis . . . and Do You Really Want to Know?

LENGTH: 3,000 words

DELIVERY: 45 days from time of assignment

WRITER: Samuel Peters (clips enclosed)

Article Treatment:

Progress in identifying a person's genetic predisposition to disease is fast outpacing society's efforts to cope with the effects, raising all manner of ethical and legal issues. Prominent among them is whether someone with a family history of a fatal genetic disorder that generally strikes in middle age (amyotrophic lateral sclerosis, for one, a.k.a. Lou Gehrig's disease) should be tested for the gene in advance of any symptoms . . . the danger here being that if the result proves positive, it could lead to depression so severe as to negatively color a person's life long before the condition ever manifests itself. Another is whether the testing itself constitutes an invasion of privacy by perhaps identifying to employers and insurance companies those who would be occupational or medical risks . . . not to mention how the revelation might otherwise stigmatize men and women found to have a serious genetic deficiency. Those are but two of the several conundrums I plan to cover.

I have already solicited the cooperation of the Hastings Center, which, as you know, deals with the whole quagmire of medical ethics; the specialists there will serve as my main authorities on the subject and I'll ask them to point me to men and women who have actually been tested as well as some who have declined to submit. I've also been in touch with the National Institutes of Health and the federal disease-control people down in Atlanta, who have also agreed to cooperate in my research.

As sidebars, I'm prepared to deliver either or both of the following:

- An explanation of the process of genetic testing.
- The counseling available to men and women who have been tested and so, in effect, know their fate.

You may have additional thoughts on the subject, in which case I'd be pleased to discuss them with you. In any event, I'd appreciate your response fairly soon, since this is a hot topic at the moment.

• If you suggest a profile—and most magazines include these in their format—of somebody big-famous, you'd better say why and how you think *you* could get to that person. *Everybody* wants to interview Madonna, Tom Cruise, Steven Spielberg. These assignments usually go to a writer with top credentials, occasionally to a friend of the celebrity. You'll have a better shot with somebody less famous.

3. Make the deal.

In the happy event that an editor has accepted your idea—with you as the writer—it's time to negotiate the deal. This is what you need to do:

• Consult the latest edition of *Writer's Market* at your local library to learn the magazine's payment scale. You'll find that most mainstream publications pay in the neighborhood of a dollar a word. Should you, as a beginning writer, be offered less, accept the suggested fee but try to extract a promise that your next assignment—if there is one—will pay the going rate. Assuming you are not writing on spec, ask for a kill fee of at least 15 percent, hardly a munificent figure when you consider that a rejected 1,500-word piece that would have paid a dollar a word will—after weeks of hard work—gross you all of $225. Certainly accept nothing less than 10 percent, or you virtually *will be* writing on spec.

• Ask what expenses are covered and the documentation needed to collect them (then be sure to save all receipts).

• Know your rights. When a magazine buys onetime rights (the most advantageous deal for the writer), you can sell the piece elsewhere after its original publication. If the deal calls for world rights, however, you cede all claim to the article forever (or, as the legalese has it, in perpetuity). At *Cosmo,* we guiltlessly buy world rights for as much material as we can, usually from writers who've had little material published. For articles from more established writers, we pay 20 percent of the original price if one or more of our international editors wants to use the material.

• Be prepared to give the magazine electronic rights for no additional payment. Until the permissions side of on-line journalism gets sorted out, the magazine is likely to insist on such rights anyway.

• If you find it uncomfortable or feel incompetent to haggle over money, you may want a literary agent to take on the task. Given the magazine's commitment, you should have no difficulty finding one. This will cost you—most likely—15 percent of your fee (or kill fee).

Advantages: The agent will bargain for the highest rate and most advantageous rights and serve as your advocate in any editorial dispute. Even with an agent, you will probably continue to submit your own article queries to magazines. Pushing your magazine work wouldn't be profitable to the agent in terms of effort and time required.

4. Request an assignment letter.

Some editors, alas, are notoriously capricious or forgetful about what you've discussed, so ask for a letter of assignment, either in addition to or in place of a contract. This assignment letter should set forth the financial terms—including expenses—deadline and details of the piece: (a) length, (b) format (Q&A, roundup, narrative with anecdotal case histories or whatever), (c) minimum number of authorities to be covered, (d) sidebar subject matter and (e) anything else you've agreed on. This letter is a bit of trouble for the assigning editor to write but is necessary, not only to serve as a guide to what you will be writing (and you'll do well to follow it assiduously), but as a reminder to the editor of precisely what he or she has ordered.

5. Become intimate with your subject.

• Whether writing a profile on a federal judge, a medical piece on mononucleosis, or an exposé of the garment trade, your initial step is to read all the available literature.

- Once you've digested your research, lived with it and made sense of it, you can begin conducting your interviews. No ad-libbing at this point: You must write down the questions you plan to ask. Be as specific as possible. Asking your subject simply to open up and tell you about himself will be as productive as asking a pussycat to roar. Your interview questions will have been created from the vast vat of knowledge that is your research.

- Most interviews are conducted with a tape recorder, augmented with written notes made at the interview. Having a taped record will save you from both lawsuits and forgetfulness about what you actually heard.

- Transcribe your tapes and review your notes as soon after an interview as possible, while memory of your conversation is still retrievable.

6. Write it right.

Once you're satisfied that your research is complete, the fun is over. The time has come to get down to the hard work of writing. Here's how to do it right.

- Make your first sentence and whole lead paragraph as clever as possible, because this opening must intrigue and lure the reader into the piece. Create interest and you'll win an audience. Be blah and you'll have no audience to lure. Don't begin an article on, say, the fiftieth anniversary of the cookies Animal Crackers with: "Come next month, Animal Crackers will celebrate its fiftieth birthday." Better to begin with "What has 178 legs and *doesn't* live under the kitchen sink?"

• You may want to write your last paragraph—known variously as the *summation,* the *wrap,* the *zinger*—next. It, too, should be clever in order to leave your audience— not to mention your editor—with the positive feeling that she or he has just had a good read and would like to hear from you again. It will also serve as a guide to get you, the writer, from the beginning to the finish line.

• Focus, focus, focus. Keep in mind your destination and you're not likely to wander too far from the main road.

• Make sure each paragraph—and certainly each sentence—is connected to the one that precedes it, that it flows out of the one before. Don't go from "Even as a neophyte actor, Clint Eastwood garnered rave reviews" to "Eastwood's first child was born in 1953." Better to follow the review statement with: "Indeed, one of Eastwood's earliest fans was his first child, born in 1953, some two years before Daddy made his screen debut."

• Quote your sources accurately as to intent but not necessarily verbatim. Remember that it's permissible— and often preferable—to clean up a source's grammar, syntax and rambling statements in order to convey a cogent thought.

• Brush up on your libel. Because libel laws in this country vary somewhat from state to state, the best advice is to adhere to the most conservative test, which in this case is: Do not say anything about a person that would make you feel embarrassed if it were said about you—unless you can prove the statement true. Put another way: Do not hold a person up to ridicule unless you have irrefutable information (legal documents) that the ridicule is warranted. As for citing previously published material, you are on safer ground quoting a prestigious source such as *The New York Times* or *Wall Street Journal* than the *National Enquirer* or *Globe*.

• Do not invade privacy. Privacy laws, too, vary from state to state, so again you'd do well to adhere to the most conservative standard, which in this area is four-pronged: Privacy is generally considered invaded if you (a) reveal private facts about a person, even though true, (b) intrude on a person's private affairs (delve into a bank account or other financial matters, say), (c) capitalize on a person's name for commercial gain or (d) cast a person in false light—that is, say something untrue about that person, even though *not* defamatory.

• Not totally necessary, but if you *want* to, following the magazine's style will make a good impression. Are numbers spelled out or expressed in figures? Are commas used before the last *and* in a series? Is spelling traditional (e.g., *catalogue, dialogue, through*) or new wave (*catalog, dialog, thru*)? Pay attention to these details and mimic them.

• Once the piece is completed, put it aside for a day or two before reviewing it. Come to the manuscript with a fresh, rested eye and you'll be amazed at the grotesqueries you'll spot, even in the most carefully conceived and written article. Yes, you can always do a little fine-tuning. Some of us write sentences, paragraphs, whole pages we thought were *there* over and over and over. Eventually, you'll know you've got it right!

• You've heard that neatness counts? It does. Use a dictionary, make sure your grammar is impeccable, double-space your copy, number your pages and proof the manuscript for any typos. I actually used to turn down manuscripts at *Cosmo* because I couldn't *read* them—single-spaced, no margins to speak of and the writer's printer badly needed ink.

7. Pay attention to the deadline.

Meet it at all costs except one: if an extension is likely to yield information that would substantially change the tone, premise or gist of the article. Suppose, say, that Sean Penn (I'm making this up) has sworn he'll never marry again, and you have pegged your piece on this vow. Then, smack against your deadline, he announces he's about to become a father once more—and, oh yes, he's marrying the mother. Your move? Ask for an extension. Failing to do so would mark you as a foolish amateur, which, at this point, you certainly are *not*!

A final word on the subject: Don't send an article you've already written on spec or even a query to more than one magazine at a time . . . you have to wait for an answer. How long? Three weeks would be a reasonable time before you call to ask what's happening; probably, you'll deal with an assistant. And yes, *always* enclose a stamped, self-addressed envelope with anything you want returned if not accepted.

Go get 'em, tiger! (Oh dear, is that a cliché?!)

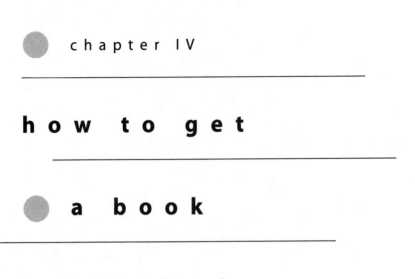

how to get

a book

published

Somebody in publishing once said that forty million people want to write a book, and only forty people want to read one! The situation isn't quite that bad. Despite the decline in readership and scale-backs on the part of publishers, an estimated seven thousand titles are still put out in hardcover by mainstream houses each year, approximately 50 percent of them by first-time authors.

Amid the flurry of rejected manuscripts (some 80 percent submitted through agents and perhaps 95 percent submitted cold), the roster of first-time-out successes is still impressive. Look at Jean Auel, a writer from the Pacific Northwest who got the attention of agent Jean Naggar nearly two decades ago and, under Naggar's guidance, went on to sell what would become her megahit, *Clan of the Cave Bear,* to Crown. Or James Redfield, whose first novel, *The Celestine Prophecy,* made the rounds of mainstream houses before the author decided, in 1993, to publish it himself (not a recommended route; although it gets you to your destination, the cost can be prohibitive). But that's just the beginning of Redfield's saga. The novel sold one hundred thousand copies in the self-published version, then was picked up by Warner Books the following year and brought out in hardcover, shot to the top of *The New York Times* bestseller list, where it remained for 165 weeks, meanwhile being anointed the number one international bestseller of 1996.

Or take Brad Meltzer, a student at Columbia Law School when he sent his first novel to fifteen agents before Jill Kneerim of the Boston-based Palmer & Dodge Agency agreed to represent him. In the end, that book garnered twenty-four rejections and was never published. But *The Tenth Justice,* his second novel, when half written, was shopped around by Kneerim, bought by Bantam, eventually published (in 1997) by William Morrow after the acquiring editor switched houses—and it has gone on to earn big money for Meltzer. More recently, thirty-four-year-old Karin Goodwin of Tucson, Arizona, was fortunate enough to have her first novel, *Sleeping with Random Beasts,* surface from the slush at Chronicle—one of the few publishers that continues to read unsolicited manuscripts (most publishers, alas, no longer do, although many are reluctant to admit it). Then, compounding her good fortune, both Barnes & Noble and Borders featured Goodwin as a "new discovery" when the book was published in March 1998.

Do you have the talent to be among the lucky first-time authors? If you've never written anything more creative than an expense account, it's hard to tell. But should you happen to have something that *looks* like ability, the best way to determine whether you've got the right stuff is to show your work to just about anyone willing to read it: a friendly librarian, guest lecturer at a writers' conference (he may not be thrilled . . . gets a lot of these requests), your old fifth-grade teacher at P.S. 987, a friend who gobbles books and might just know publishable if he or she saw it. Ask them all to be candidly critical, then listen—really listen—to what they have to say. "I can't count the number of horror stories I hear about the years that are lost, the spirits that are crushed because people choose not to heed the words 'You're no good at writing, do something else'—even though they've asked for a frank opinion," says Joni Evans, a senior vice president at the William Morris agency.

fiction

Let's start with fiction. How do you go about getting your work into the right hands? It's not easy but definitely doable. The submission process for a first work of fiction used to be that the writer would send a finished manuscript to either a publisher or an agent and hope the novel would rise from the slush pile. That was when reading the slush was assigned to the most junior editor or agent. Now that unsolicited manuscripts go largely unread, the rule no longer applies. Indeed, rare is the editor (or agent, if you're also going that route—see number

2 on page 52) who wants to see more than a letter—a bright, fresh, succinct, provocative, enticing letter describing the plot—sent exclusively to one publisher at a time. Address your correspondence to a specific editor at a publishing house—more in a moment about finding the house and editor. Keep the letter short and to the point. Then she or he, if interested, will ask to see a few chapters, and if those seem promising, you'll be asked for the completed manuscript. "The last thing I want is to have a whole book arrive on my desk uninvited," says Betty Prashker, executive vice president and editor-at-large at Crown. "I'd much rather read a pithy letter and then ask for more material if I'm intrigued." That same pithy letter should also be submitted simultaneously to as many agents as you can connect with (again, see number 2 on page 52) in the hope that it will intrigue one of them as well.

nonfiction

Here's the way to acquire the know-how needed to get yourself published in this area, or at least read by the pros who count (the process is in some ways similar to selling a magazine article; you'll quickly pick up the parallels).

1. Research the market.
Not everybody goes this route—that is, determining what's already out there in the marketplace on *your* sub-

ject and how the books are doing—but it doesn't hurt to follow it. The best place to research is in the marketplace itself, specifically a bookstore. Say you want to write a book on ballet through the ages. Browse among the shelves at your local bookstore; you'll see what's currently being stocked and, presumably, sold. (Other books on ballet may be in print but not currently carried by the store.) Perhaps four of the titles you find will be under the Harmony Books imprint, a division of Random House—ergo, probably the best publisher for books on ballet. A glance at the subtitles will reveal the territory already covered, the new ground left for you to break. (That any number of books are out there on your subject shouldn't discourage you; just be sure to take a different tack, approach the material from a new angle.) Although nothing may dissuade you from going forward with *your* book (because yours will be different and a masterpiece!), you might chat up the store manager during hours when she or he isn't too busy to learn how well the category is selling.

Toward finding an agent, the bookstore browse could also be useful. Many authors thank people who have helped them with their work, and an agent's name is often among those acknowledgments in the front of the book. Later, you'd check the *Literary Market Place (LMP),* a book available at your local library, which lists, among other things, literary agencies and the people who work there. Among all the agencies and listed personnel, perhaps you'll find the one in the acknowledgments who was so helpful to a writer on your particular subject, and you can then address a letter to him or her. (See number 2.)

The Sunday *New York Times Book Review* section does brief reviews of many books just being published—another source of information about activity within your subject and who's publishing what. A third excellent source of information about books already written on your subject is the *Books in Print* series, available at your local library. Its volumes are arranged variously according to title, author, subject matter—subject matter at this stage being the one you'll want to consult. (Maybe there won't have been *any* books published on your particular subject, but that isn't likely.) Then, for the names and addresses of the publishers who seem to have a penchant for your sort of book (let's say Doubleday has published six on big-time irregularities in the legal profession), you can consult the *LMP*—the source book just mentioned in connection with tracking an agent . . . it contains a lot of stuff! The latest edition on my shelf devotes 270 pages to legitimate publishers (along with names and titles of the editors at each house)—from AACC Press in Washington, D.C., to Zone Books in New York City.

If, in researching books on your subject in *Books in Print* and at your local bookstore and consulting the Sunday *New York Times Book Review* to see what's just come out, a particular publisher doesn't strike you as any more promising than another, you'll just have to take a chance! Many publishers are eclectic anyway and no more partial to one subject than another. As you read names of legitimate publishers in the *LMP,* you'll somehow pick one with whom to start your literary journey. I can't tell you which *editor* to choose from those listed at a particular house—wouldn't be the CEO or editor in chief. Any senior editor should be fine.

2. Write a proposal.

This step along the path to publication is to books what the query is to articles: When properly executed, the proposal will sell both you and your idea to a publisher—and, not incidentally, to an agent as well. The difference is that while magazine queries follow a fairly rigid format, book proposals are much more flexible in nature. But if there are, essentially, no rules to govern a proposal's breadth or length, tips to maximize effectiveness abound. Here are a few.

• At minimum—and many editors prefer the *barest* minimum; it saves them so much time when all they want initially is to be grabbed by an idea—a proposal should include an overview of the subject matter (a *brief* synopsis of the story you plan to tell, the point of view you'll take), the way you intend to present the material (chronologically by decade, perhaps, if you're going to write about the hundred-year evolution of fashion from bustle to funk couture), a note about the competition (how many other books have been done on the topic and how yours will differ from them), why you are particularly qualified to tackle this project.

Here is an example of a brief but eminently adequate proposal (with made-up facts, figures and fictitious names):

TITLE: Have You Lived Before?

SUBTITLE: When Past Lives Come Back to Haunt—and Help—You!

AUTHOR: Arden Spathe

OVERVIEW:

A pseudoscientific investigation (with the author as guinea pig) into the otherwordly realm of reincarnation, the ancient philosophy rooted in Buddhism and Hinduism that is currently soaring to New Age heights . . . a philosophy that posits how the soul survives death and returns to Earth time and again, on each occasion in a new body.

TREATMENT:

Unlike the volumes written by Edgar Cayce and Shirley MacLaine, or any of the twenty-five other books on the subject still in print, mine will tell how I, dubious but curious about past-life claims, underwent one hundred sessions of hypnotic regression with Alfred Devline, noted psychiatrist and prominent member of the American Society for Past-Life Research. Chapter by chapter, I will detail the seven most dramatic lives I came to experience while in a deep meditative state: a twelfth-century Spanish sailor lost at sea, a nineteenth-century English prostitute, a Puritan church elder who killed himself in disgrace when his daughter was violated by a rapist, an early twentieth-century physician who died miserably of bubonic plague, a ballerina in Revolutionary Russia, an embittered magician in seventeenth-century France set on avenging his wife's infidelity, and an early Wagnerian soprano of some promise who was horribly disfigured in a backstage fire.

POINT OF VIEW:

Am I still skeptical of reincarnation, or am I convinced that I have lived before? Perhaps I can best answer that question by quoting Voltaire: "It is not more surprising to be born twice than once; everything in nature is resurrection." What I *am* unequivocally certain of is that my brush with past-life regression has made me better understand what my purpose is in life today.

If my idea appeals, I can have a more detailed outline on your desk in a matter of days, along with a few chapters if that's what you'd like. I'm also, of course, open to any suggestions you might have that would make the book a more viable publishing project. Can we talk?

———

• You may choose to enhance the proposal by including an outline, which can be a strong selling point, especially if your idea is somewhat esoteric. Take a book on music in ancient Greece, not high on everyone's must-read list: By detailing, chapter by chapter, the evolution of the art form (Chapter 1: The Monodic Era: No Harmony in the Ancient World . . . Chapter 3: Homer and the Golden Age of Musical Culture . . . Chapter 7: Choral Music Comes to Tragedy . . . Chapter 12: Play It Again Pythagoras: From Phorminx to Aulos to Kithara), you just may tweak the curiosity of an editor whose prior interest in the subject was nil and possibly impress him or her with your command of the material.

• You may also want to include a sample chapter, although many in the business strongly advise that it's best to wait until (and *if*) asked—the theory here being that it's more profitable to tantalize step-by-step than to overwhelm a busy editor with voluminous proof of your talent for the written word.

• Or you may prefer—at your peril, some editors caution—to submit a proposal so detailed that it can serve not only as an overview but eventually the first two or three chapters.

• Under no circumstances should you actually write a book, start to finish, before seeking a publisher . . . not only to avoid a dreadful waste of time but to spare yourself the heartbreak of being told there is no market for all your months—maybe years—of hard work.

• Don't worry about a title. Although on rare occasions a book has been bought merely on the basis of its title being irresistible, the chances of an author coming up with the perfect header is perhaps 25 percent. The guideline here: While a great title at the proposal stage is a valuable selling tool, it's preferable to submit a proposal with, say, the heading "Untitled on Greek Music" rather than to tack on one that's bad.

• In the end, the writing is all. You could be suggesting the most innovative idea to come along since ATMs, but if the presentation is dull, the subject will just lie there, flat on the page, and its greatness will go unrecognized. Conversely, you could be dealing with a subject as witless as anything dredged up from the bottom of the gene pool, and if the treatment is imaginative, your voice exciting—yes, an editor can often tell, even from a *brief* proposal—you're likely to get an enthusiastic response . . . at the very least, an invitation to meet with the publisher to perhaps massage the idea into a more viable shape.

3. Get an agent.

While you can, of course, trek solo through the various stages of publishing—in which case we'll hope a specific editor in the publishing house you're interested in is interested in your book—agents do make invaluable traveling companions. Hook up with one if you can. Besides submitting your proposal to the appropriate house and making the initial deal with a publisher on your behalf, a good literary agent will (a) market your book in foreign countries and to movies and magazines, (b) keep a vigilant eye on every aspect of the publishing process, (c) offer editorial advice . . . perhaps even put a pencil to your manuscript, (d) hold your hand when necessary and otherwise boost your morale, (e) help fight your publishing battles, or, barring that, lend you moral support.

If you've written a fairly good proposal, finding an agent isn't all that difficult, despite warnings to the contrary. Remember having culled agent names from those acknowledgments in books on your subject and agency addresses from the *LMP* at your public library (listed right after publishers—thirty-five pages of names and addresses, from the Aachen Group in Ridgecrest, California, to George Ziegler in New York). Now's the time to use them: In a cover letter attached to your proposal, tell the agent that, say, "I'm a particular fan of Roger Caras, and I, too, as you'll see, am writing about animals. I noticed in the acknowledgments in his last book that you're his agent, and . . ." blah, blah, blah. That one simple letter may be all that's necessary to rescue your proposal from the slush. If you didn't find any agent acknowledged in books on your subject or can't tell whether any of the names in the acknowledgments *be-*

long to an agent, just pick somebody's name from those listed under agencies in *LMP,* and, when you send in your proposal, make no reference to specific authors he or she might have helped because you won't know who they are.

An alternative tack is to go begging, proposal in hand, to any acquaintance, however remote, who might have some connection to an agent or publisher. During my years as *Cosmo* editor, I got a letter approximately every two weeks asking if I could read a book manuscript or proposal, help the writer find an agent or a publisher. I couldn't. The magazine would never have got to the printer if I had, but I didn't scoff at the people who tried. I told you about writing my first book, *Sex and the Single Girl,* because I was scared and frustrated in a copywriting job at the Kenyon & Eckhardt advertising agency where two wonderful young women, Mary Louise Lau and Marilyn Hart, and I were given the same assignments on the Max Factor account and were, if friends, also rivals. We'd all be turned loose to do television spots for a Pink Jade promotion, print copy for High Society lipstick and Primitif perfume and name new products . . . we each had a list of hundreds. My storyboards for commercials never made it to film, and precious little print copy got printed. All of us uneasy, Marilyn, Mary Louise and I occasionally snuck off to the Pantages Theatre next door—Hollywood and Vine—to let Ruby Gentry and Spartacus soothe our psyches. Our shared secretary was told we were conferring. Having three people turned loose on every assignment was not only wasteful but also didn't make for job security, as I mentioned. David thought of a book idea for me—what it was like to be single. Keeping my day job, as they say, I went to work on my ancient manual typewriter that spoke Spanish, with some symbols that don't exist in English (it was a leave-behind from one of David's former wives . . . she didn't leave much). David didn't help with the direction of the book but at times would look at what I'd written, reject . . . "not there yet."

Nobody knows the drafts that were drafted for the first chapter—a kind of rah, rah, rah for being single— or of the subsequent *very* detailed outline of the other chapters: of sex, careers, the apartment, entertaining, health, fashion, beauty, etc. David finally saw a draft he said would get by, did no serious editing and talked to a former book-editor friend now prowling Hollywood trying to get a movie job. Saul suggested we send the book to his former employer, Oscar Dystal of Bantam Books, then only a paperback house, but getting the manuscript considered by *anybody* who could publish was more important to David and me than what kind of publishing it was. Bantam turned it down. What a night that was in the Polo Lounge of the Beverly Hills Hotel, where the rejecters broke the news, me bravely fighting back tear splashes until I got home. Oscar said they couldn't handle the book but suggested

I send it off to Bernard Geis and Associates, a new publisher with few titles to his credit—this was no Alfred Knopf or Scribner's, but somebody who might take a chance on such a kooky book. Berney's letter saying he'd take it came to the office. People have asked occasionally what were the happiest moments of my life. Getting that letter from Berney had to be in the top five. Yes, thousands of books are published every year—*thousands!* but this was *my* book . . . miracle time for somebody writing for so long without even a magazine article in print. Letty Cottin Pogrebin, a towheaded, barely-past-teenage publicist in Berney's office, was the one who banged on him to buy.

Bernard Geis was perfect because he believed in me, printed and managed to get Random House to distribute enough copies so the book would be available in stores when promotion kicked in. Berney was the first publisher to promote authors through radio and television— that is, get you on and back on anything in radio and television that would let you talk your brains out—as well as scrounge print interviews. Berney's next first-time-out find was Jacqueline Susann, whose *Every Night Josephine* and *Valley of the Dolls* were published with max success. Everybody doesn't have the advantage of pushy and somewhat connected husbands like Jackie and me, but any recommendation, even from the principal of your high school alma mater, will open more doors than no recommendation at all.

No agent was involved with publication of *Sex and the Single Girl*, nor did I use one for the next four books. Many years later, Irving Paul "Swiftly" Lazar represented *Having It All* and later *The Late Show*. *Having It All* was a *New York Times* bestseller. *The Late Show* (about being older) was originally contracted for by Random House; the editor, however, didn't think it had enough of a feminist slant and wanted massive changes. I had no wish to do that, so Irving took the book to another publisher, William Morrow, which bought it immediately. Yes, agents can be blessings, though I didn't have one for my first five books; Bernard Geis and Avon Books (a Hearst Corporation softcover imprint) did all of them.

So, back to my first baby. We started promotion immediately. I wasn't a performer, but the subject matter—okay to be single and have a sex life—was so delicious for its time lots of people wanted to talk to me, and I seemed to have a knack for expressing "outrageous" opinions. As many book-writing amateur performers have found, you never *know* how well you can do until they pin a microphone on you. My first big interview was on the *Today* show, with its book critic, Cleveland Amory. Cleveland told his audience I was incapable of writing a dull word . . . wasn't that nice? I remember coming out into the sunshine at Rockefeller Plaza, smiling like a monkey, heading straight for the bookstores. Mercifully, smart Berney had convinced them to take enough copies and sales started immediately . . . heady!

Sex and the Single Girl was subsequently bought by Warner Bros. and made into a movie with Natalie Wood playing me as a psychiatrist! Tony Curtis, Henry Fonda and Lauren Bacall also starred. I had nothing to do with the screenplay. Take the money and run, said my smart husband, who'd had experience with nonexperienced book writers trying to get involved with screenplays. Baby glitch: Jack Warner had been interested in the book because his girlfriend, Jackie Parks, had told him about it, probably during pillow talk. "Jack," she had said, "You've never read anything like this in your life . . . you've got to buy it!" Buy it he did, read it he didn't. On actually reading his purchase, Mr. Warner got a little hysterical. "I've bought a goddamned bunch of recipes!" he declared. (For sexy little dinners, Jack.) "And [unprintable] beauty secrets!" (The better to look good at dinner, Jack.) Glitch unglitched. Warners turned a writer loose who constructed a plot and a wonderful movie was made, still shown on television. Warners and we subsequently sued Albert Ellis and his publisher, Lyle Stuart, because Albert had quickly written *Sex and the Single Man,* and Warners said the studio had too much at stake with its movie for a producer to come along, buy just any book for the title and make a movie called *Sex and the Single Man.* We won the lawsuit.

Let me tell you a little about post–book publication, because it could happen to *you*. What do we call it, instant celebrity? Most friends were wonderful, some a little sniffy. The money ($200,000 for the movie rights) bothered Margaret. "Hello, rich girl," she would always open the conversation. A psychiatrist pal was *furious*. Lunching with me at the Brown Derby, he said, "Helen, how could you write a book of advice for women when you have had no training, no credentials whatever . . . that was irresponsible!" I left him with his Cobb salad at the Derby; haven't seen him since. The book brought an avalanche of mail, mentioned earlier. At one point the post office in Pacific Palisades wouldn't even deliver it, but we would have to go to the post office to pick it up. During the book hullabaloo, David left Twentieth-Century Fox. The studio had closed because of losses on *Cleopatra*, but let's not go into that. We moved to New York. The *Sex and the Single Girl* mail was still pouring in. I've told you about how the book and all the mail brought the creation of (new) *Cosmo*. Now let's get back to you (finally!). We were talking about finding somebody to help you get a book published and subsequent considerations. Shall we continue? A word of caution here about literary lawyers: Although there are a few who excel and serve as effectively as the best literary agents in every step of the publishing process, the majority are at their best as authors' representatives when negotiating the contract but may lag behind in the follow-through—foreign sales, for one, or the marketing of subsidiary rights.

4. Hold out for your rights.

- Primary and most prominent: Tell your agent not to give away world rights; they have become extremely lucrative in recent years. Unless your book is so peculiarly American in subject matter as to preclude any interest abroad, do not cede these rights to your publisher.

- The second most lucrative rights to retain are audio rights (talking books); there is absolutely no reason why a publisher should automatically own them.

- Also insist on retaining electronic rights, except for the electronic book (i.e., an exact replica of the book in disk form). Any electronic mix of your book with material from elsewhere is considered multimedia and the rights to such should not automatically belong to the publisher.

- Movie and film rights don't present much of a fight, because publishers almost never expect to own them.

- Although the author generally retains first-serial rights (which pertain mainly to prepublication excerption by magazines), some agents advise their clients to turn these over to the publisher on the theory that holding—and ultimately selling—such rights energizes the house, gives everyone from editor to promotion staff to sales-people a more intimate feeling of involvement in the book's success, imparts a jolt of enthusiasm that can pay off handsomely for the author—and the agent too.

5. Don't be a royal (ties) pain.

Once you've signed the contract, let your agent handle any dispute, particularly if it has to do with money. And to preempt confusion, learn up front the advance/royalties system. Here's how it works:

• The publisher agrees to pay you a certain fee in advance of publication, the money to be applied against future earnings of your book. This sum, known as the *advance,* will come to you in installments: perhaps half on signing the contract and half on acceptance of the finished manuscript . . . or maybe one third on signing, one third on delivery of the first half of the book, and the remaining third on acceptance of the completed manuscript.

• All money the publisher earns from your book by selling the rights that the house owns (book club rights, say, or paperback, second serial, whatever) is credited to your advance.

• A percentage of the price of each copy of your book that's sold is also credited to your advance. This percentage is known as the *royalty* and is fairly standard in the industry (for hardcover: 10 percent of the book's price is paid to the author for each of the first 5,000 copies sold,

12.5 percent from 5,001 to 10,000 and 15 percent therafter).

• Once—and if—your advance is earned out (meaning the publishing company has earned back the money it advanced to you), you can expect to receive royalty checks periodically based on the above percentages. Part of your agent's job is to make sure these checks, when due, are forthcoming. Should there be any disagreement in this area, do not become involved directly; let your agent fight the battle.

6. Ask what your editor can do for you and what you can do for your editor.

The first thing you can do is pray that the editor who signed you up will still be with the house by the time you turn in your finished manuscript. As for what to expect from her or him, that varies. Many editors are actually collaborators: They become involved in the organization of a manuscript, the shaping of it, the line editing, etc. Most solid houses still have editors of this type—but these days, there are fewer solid houses. If you happen to be in the hands of a hands-*off* editor, you may want to hire a freelance person to help. These people exist, and your editor at the publishing house can probably recommend somebody.

The house is also supposed to perform the legal vetting of your manuscript, but sometimes the person assigned this task gives a naïve reading or simply can't handle the volume. You'd do well to be vigilant in your research and writing, especially because you, as the author, will be responsible for paying the first $100,000 (at which point the publisher's insurance kicks in) of any judgment found against you for reasons of libel, invasion of privacy, plagiarism or infringement of copyright (you are responsible as well for obtaining permission to use any copyrighted material).

Know, too, that it's always prudent to meet your deadline: More and more these days, publishers are bailing out of the deal and demanding a return of the advance when an author misses a deadline and exceeds the automatic three-month extension.

7. Be extracurricularly active, but carefully so.

The degree of your involvement in the fringe stuff—jacket selection, flap and catalogue copy, marketing, promotion—should lie somewhere between *as much as you're allowed* and *as little as possible*. In effect, your participation in this area is a little like dating: Woman or man, you have to be adorable and helpful and undemanding, all the while wooing the publisher into letting you set the relationship right if it threatens to go somewhat off. Which is to say, if something really seems wrong to you, you ought to be able to exercise veto power. But don't expect that to be necessary. You are, after all, dealing with professionals who have a lot more know-how than a smattering of cynics would have you believe. Publishers are in the *business* of selling books, and, as one of their valued authors, you should trust that they'll do the right thing.

Can't wait for you to hit the bookstores *and The New York Times* bestseller list.

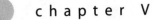

chapter V

how to

write a

good letter

aside from business letters, complaining-about or asking-for-something letters we all have to write at times, hasn't "old-fashioned," non–E-mail, non-fax letter-writing pretty much gone out of style? Not for some of us. Having started writing letters at age six, I never let up . . . I told you about that and about the thriller letter from Bernard Geis saying he'd publish my book . . . a life changer. I write dozens of letters a week and people sometimes tell me they save my letters because they make them feel good. There! That's one reason to write. Do you know anyone who doesn't fish through the daily junk mail hoping to find, longing for, a little personal note from a friend? The late composer Burton Lane told me he was sloshing through junk mail one day, saw a Hearst Corporation envelope, figured it was a solicitation of some kind, sliced it open anyway—surprise! it's *me* telling him how much we'd all thrilled to Tony Bennett's singing "You're All the World to Me" and "Too Late Now" from Burton and Alan Jay Lerner's magical score for the movie *Royal Wedding* at a benefit the night before. The composer said he smiled all day. *You* can—should—

make people smile, too. I recently got a darling letter from somebody I didn't know who made *me* smile.

> Dear Helen Gurley Brown,
> It is with more warm and sincere thanks than words can express—re: your lovely signed photo—which is prominently displayed in a silver frame above my work station at home! Glancing up at your photo each day reminds me of what can be accomplished—today I have signed a contract for my novel—historical fiction—it has taken me fourteen years and eleven rejections—finally acceptance thanks to your inspiration.
> God bless

Aside from writing smile letters, a letter with a request, particularly to somebody hard to land, can be more effective than telephoning. In writing you can be gracious, persuasive, specific and un-nervous, plus the recipient has a chance to think things over. Writing can actually take less time than telephoning. You know the drill. You can't get through to the wanted one, leave a message (messages), wait for the call back that doesn't come, you're going nuts . . . Write! My request letters frequently get what they ask for, so maybe I'm not the worst person to give advice. Rules for writing letters that go in envelopes also work for E-mail, although we aren't E-mailing love or condolence letters just *yet*! Here are a few thoughts.

general rules for writing letters

1. Short is usually better than long, not just for business and asking-for-something letters but personal ones as well. Does the recipient really want a ten-page account of your and Aaron's trip to the Grand Canyon or to know what your five grandchildren have been up to since Christmas? Report the news, don't drone. Short is particularly important if you are trying to persuade the recipient to do what you want him to do or are writing to somebody "over your head"—celebrity, business biggie, public official, etc.

2. Type or word-process business letters, of course. The handwritten note, thought to be "proper" for personal thank-yous, I haven't written in years . . . my handwriting is too hard to read and typing is faster, though I enjoy six-line "personals" from other people. Do what works for you. What people want is to *hear* from you . . . nobody cares about 1927 etiquette guidelines. If you do handwrite, leave space between sentences, don't write on both sides of the paper unless it's bond. Double-, even triple-spaced, typed letters are easier to read. Leave decent margins.

3. Stationery should be bond paper for business letters; anything goes for personal—only brides showing off their new status can be forgiven for insisting on engraved Cartier vellum—it's your choice.

4. No angry or hate letters, please. As others have ad-

vised, if you write the angry letter, hold it a day or two—maybe you'll talk yourself out of sending it. Really pissed? Need a wrong righted? You'll still be more effective writing calm than angry. Through all the years at *Cosmo* I never read the hate, or even disapproving, mail. It couldn't help me produce a better magazine. I was doing what I thought was right, putting out the product I believed in; sales figures corroborated my convictions—why suffer hurt feelings and aggravation from "angry"? In thirty-two years I think I've written just two angry letters, both to reporters when I was leaving my job as editor of U.S. *Cosmo* to become international editor, both of whom got the facts screwed up and were so hateful I thought they "deserved" more than a mere fact-correcting letter. I'll let you write two in thirty-two years!

5. Writing style: Some instructors advise short sentences for most of our output; at least throw in short ones between the long. Ernest Hemingway, a Nobel and Pulitzer Prize–winning genius, was the master of short/pithy. I can't quite go along with Ernest and the short/pithy advisers, though I interrupt long sentences with dashes and dots, put things in parentheses, underscore words to keep sentences alive. What we want in letter writing is friendly, no tensing up, please, just because you're writing instead of talking. In business correspondence, if you're getting wordy you might cut out a sentence or two or condense. I do that. And how can you argue with *these* two notions?

___

• Write the thank-you letter *now*. What's needed is your response, not brilliance. *What* you say doesn't even matter that much, just write!

• Send the fan letter. Everybody out there's waiting to hear from you.

thank-you letters

As I said, it almost doesn't matter *what* you write, only *that* you write. Who hasn't called Tiffany's to see if the goblets ever actually got out of the store; the secretary whose boss and wife you sent a Christmas plum pudding, it's now February, no word . . . did they move to Borneo? A cosmetic tycooness I know—the most generous woman alive—doesn't *do* thank-you's. I'm still waiting to hear about the pure silk Indonesian sari I sent months ago I'd really like to have kept for myself, not always the case with my presents. Chloe is into giving, not thanking. You only need to thank the way you talk—what's to get all tensed up about? "Dear Gene, a whole *case* of Arizona grapefruit . . . what a neat present! Love and kisses, Ray." Or a smidge more detailed: "Sue and I are having grapefruit sliced, juiced, sectioned, left in the shell, baked with Cointreau. It's great to have enough grapefruit for a feeding frenzy." The simplest note will do for flowers or a plant. "The azalea is so beautiful . . . full of pink blossoms . . . it's sitting on the coffee table wowing everybody. Thanks so much . . . lots of love, Alice."

Watch it a little with "It's so nice you were thinking about me" instead of mentioning the specific present. As someone who isn't into gifting Prada handbags or Hermès ties, I've received a few of those "thought that counts" thank-you letters—dead giveaway the present, possibly a passalong, was just as tacky as you were afraid it was! Even for a gift you can't be enthusiastic about, you have to try to be gracious. Saying you are actually wearing or using a present is good. "The magenta and orange scarf is around my neck this minute . . . it's so pretty." "I've got a picture of Aleta, Robin and Jo Jo (the cocker spaniel) in the frame and it's on my desk . . . they all look great." Lying is fine. Probably nobody is going to show up at your house to find Jo Jo, Robin and Aleta aren't on your desk like you said . . . maybe you moved them to the office. For host or hostess, a few specifics about the party are welcome. "Did you bring the boeuf bourguignon recipe back from Provence? As you may have noticed, I had two Eiffel Tower–size portions." "Thanks for putting me next to Judd Gottschalk . . . I've always wanted to meet him . . . are you a good friend or *what*?!" Tell the party giver he or she looked great. "Beverly, you were radiant! How did you *do* that when you had sixteen hungry people to feed . . . sumptuously?!" "Jerry, is it the golf? You're skinnier than when we met sixteen years ago and everything surrounding the skinny looks great . . . I think I hate you!" Admire the house or apartment. "What a place! The minute we got home Lydia walked me into the living room and said 'We've got to redecorate . . . Paul has these couches', etc. etc."

Always safe to tell the host or hostess he or she gives the *best* parties . . . he or she hopes it's true and likes corroboration. To acknowledge a present *or* party, *smile* is a word I like a lot. "The present [party, flowers, evening] is making me smile."

These are recent thank-you notes I've received that I liked.

Dear Helen,

I'm so glad the Chardonnay turned out to be vinegar and your guilty conscience made you come up with two bottles of Château Margaux Premier Grand Cru Classé . . . quel replacement! When you brought the Chardonnay originally and said if it wasn't still good, tell you, I wouldn't have, but you asked again last week and I felt you really wanted to know. The upgrade is a killer, to put it mildly. We had a bottle last night with Timmy home from St. Lawrence and are saving the next for something big . . . maybe you'll come over and we'll toast your guilty conscience! All our thanks . . .

Love,
Tom

Dear Helen and David,

Many thanks for a wonderful, fun dinner. Helen, you

look absolutely fabulous. You look pretty damn good too, David. If you two, at any point, split up, I would be delighted to have Helen live with me in California. I am sure I could find a place somewhere for David too. I do hope we will get together soon. You are great friends and great company. With affection to you both,

    Luff,

    Ray

Isn't this a super letter from George Lang, owner of Café des Artistes restaurant in New York? His biography, *Nobody Knows the Truffles I've Seen,* knocked me totally out and I wrote him.

Dear Helen,

I haven't written a love letter since the day I met Jenifer (in my office as she was doing a freelance interview with me for the *Times*), but I think I will break this seventeen-year record. Even though the publication of my book is six weeks away, I have already received terrific reviews in *Publishers Weekly* and in the *Kirkus Reviews* as well as flattering calls, letters and missives from people whose word I respect. But, none of them truly appreciated my work the way I hoped it would be read and for that reason your letter was especially joyful and important for me. By now there are gauges to measure just about everything; there is even a nilometer, an instrument for measuring the rise in the Nile during its periodic flooding, but, gauging literary quality, the flavor of language and the juiciness of a punchline can only be measured by someone like you and this certainly deserves a letter of gratitude and affection.

Jenifer and I send you and David our warmest regards,
George

Nice thank-you letter from *Today* show movie critic Gene Shalit for his birthday present:

Dear Helen:

Someone has left on my doorstep the most wonderful cuddly scrumptious lovable luxurious peppy perky languid pooch from an obviously fine canine family and he is clearly the pick of the litter. I have taken him in, dished up tasty treats, pampered him, and given him the best seat in the house. He is a sure thing to win next year's *Best in Show* ribbon at the Westminster Kennel Club Show. I have always wanted a brown dog and now my dreams have come true: Not only is *he* brown but I am certain beyond doubt he was presented to me by a certain Helen Gurley Brown, with highly exuberant support from another great Brown, Sir David by name.

I send you both a deep bow. . . .
and a cheerful bow wow
of

Thanks.

Gene

The University of Georgia recently celebrated what would have been the hundredth birthday of native son Nunnally Johnson (screenplays: *Grapes of Wrath, Tobacco*

Road, Three Faces of Eve, How to Marry a Millionaire, etc.), which David attended. Nunnally's widow, Dorris, saw David and me on CNN's *Pinnacle* and wrote:

> Dear, dear ones—
> I sat grinning like a Cheshire cat at the infernal machine a few nites ago. You two super achievers took your accolades so modestly I began to stomp 'n' whistle, about all that's left for us commoners to do.
> Clearly, Helen, the moon was pulling harder on your side of the river than on mine. I grew up a few miles away from your birthplace, in Memphis. All I have to show for that is a faded, wrinkled stretch of tacky ribbon saying "Miss Memphis." It got me to Atlantic City and a first sight of New York and that's all. It was enough. Even with your stack of creditable achievements, I now wish you more 'n' more.
> As for you, Mistah David, I cannot forget the joy I felt when I saw you in Columbus. I feared only me and my brood would be there and not one of us had any idea what we would do. You gave it all such stature, distinction. A truly great filmmaker was among us. He gave a genuine salute to an old and respected friend.
> Did I kiss you for doing and being that special person? Well when I next see you I'll do just that 'n' that 'n' that. Please show up soon.
> Dorris
> (Dorris is eighty-four)

My own best experience from writing fan letters is possibly my friendship with Woody Allen. When he performed as a young stand-up comedian at the Blue Angel in New York in the sixties, David and I were devotees. I didn't send letters but once threw a hard roll *hard* at somebody at the next table who was talking during his act and told that person to shut up. When Woody began to direct movies, I sent fan letters to his office always detailing *why* I thought the films were wonderful, described scenes, quoted dialogue . . . I made notes with a flashlight at my seat. About six years ago I started asking Woody for screenings of my own for New York shakers and loved ones; he has let me screen his last five movies. (I continue to run *Everyone Says I Love You* about once a month at home). Somehow I know the screening largesse has come from my longtime (*sincere*) fan-letter writing, and, yes, I got more famous and could get his attention. When Woody married Soon-Yi, I wrote (we never had *had* conversations!) to ask if he would like me to give a small dinner party so Soon-Yi could meet some grownups. He said yes . . . sweet little party—fourteen people—at our pretty apartment, kind of a fabulous night—I credit fan-letter writing. A bottle of 1990 Château Lafite-Rothschild accompanied the thank-you note.

And from a bride:

Dear DB and HGB,
    Your "timing" is AMAZING! Your wonderful, beautiful gift could not have been more welcome! I don't

know whether you know but we have been redecorating the master bedroom. Last week our new bedside tables came in and suddenly the table clock Ernie had had in the bedroom looked too shabby for the "new look." I brought a clock from my apartment, but that didn't do justice to the room either. So yesterday, when I went on my annual full-day "getting ready for Christmas" shopping trek, Ernie and I talked about my keeping an eye out for a table clock for the bedroom. I was sure that somewhere, during the entire day, I would find *something*. Nope! I came home defeated. But, when I arrived, there was your package. And, I gasped when we opened it. There it was: the perfect clock for our side table! It's even brass—just like all the hardware and sconces and lamps in the room. So, many, many thanks for making our redecorating easy, and accomplishing what I could not! Best of all, we will be looking at this clock several times a day, which will bring the two of you to mind every time!

Love,

Laurie

Okay, you can forget every one of these suggestions except one: Do write quickly to say thank you!

complaint letters

We all have to complain occasionally. Keep in mind you want the recipient of your complaint letter to make good on something, not just to listen to you moan. If there isn't something you actually *want,* you could probably skip the letter. Toward getting satisfaction, try to be a *little* diplomatic; even a touch of flattery couldn't hurt. We don't want your letter tossed in the wastebasket with the recipient recoiling from an ugly attack.

Write to a specific person. From the menu of possible extensions you will get when telephoning a big—or even small—company, this won't be easy. Be persistent. When a live operator finally comes on the line, say you need the name of customer-service director or whomever you have in mind. There *is* one in most companies and he's there to hear from people like you and me, especially in letters rather than by phone.

Dear Airline:
    May I tell you what happened with your airline and me last week and hope we can work something out?
    Thursday, August 21, I arrived at LAX at 8:30 A.M. to check in for flight 642 to JFK, scheduled for departure at 9:00 A.M., was told the flight was overbooked, my reservation could not be honored, you would put me on the next possible flight. That flight turned out to be 726, leaving LAX at 11:00 A.M., arriving at JFK at 8:00 P.M. New York time, two hours late for a meeting my company had scheduled at JFK at 6:00 P.M.
    I missed the meeting, which was not only an embarrassment for me but the kind of thing that could put one's job in jeopardy. The meeting went on without me,

and my not showing made me look like some kind of ditz who couldn't handle a simple plane reservation. Leaving Los Angeles at dawn to be able to attend a 6:00 P.M. meeting at the airport in New York hadn't occurred to me. Except for being bumped from my flight, a 9:00 A.M. departure should have been fine. I'm aware that, because of no-shows, airlines have to overbook. If I'd arrived at LAX at 8:50 A.M. for a 9:00 A.M. departure, perhaps that would have been cutting it a little close, but half an hour ahead of departure for a domestic flight, if not ideal, should have been sufficient time to put me on the plane. Maybe someone whose arrival in New York was not so crucial could have been asked to take a later flight in return for a bonus; I'm not aware this was done. I think you should now either (a) issue me a free coach ticket (the kind I was holding) from Los Angeles to New York or (b) upgrade me from coach to first class on several subsequent flights. Don't you want me out there saying *good* things about my favorite airline rather than bad-mouthing you to whomever I can get to listen? May I hear from you?

Dear [name of person at car company]:

My wife and I love our Leapfrog XK 375. What we don't love is the bill we had to pay ($425.00—attached) to get the window on the driver's side to roll up and down. The window was okay for six months after purchase, then got stuck. The repair shop said the one-year warranty did not cover the work because it involved the electrical system. Obviously a warranty should cover something as crucial as a window rolling up and down, particularly on the driver's side. Since I couldn't be without the car while the bill got sorted out, I paid for the repair and would now appreciate your reimbursing me.

The Leapfrog XK 375 is terrific. This is my third Leapfrog and I hope someday to buy a fourth, but I'd like the windows to work for a certain amount of time without my having to pay for repairs! I know [name of car company] wants satisfied customers. If you want to discuss this matter, my phone number is [number]. I'll look forward to hearing from you and/or receiving a check.

Sincerely,

Dear Contractor,

During the time between completion of our house at 835 N. Spruce Street and the time we were promised completion, my wife, children and I had to stay at the Holiday Inn, which cost $1,326, bill attached. I hope you will reimburse us for this. As our contractor, you guaranteed in writing completion of the house by February 28, 1998, but we were unable to move in until April 4, 1998. Based on your estimate of completion the people who bought our present house were guaranteed occupancy by February 28, so we were forced to move out. You have received from us a total of $87,562, surely a sum that can accommodate our motel bill for a period we were unable to occupy our new house. We love the house, are eager to tell others of your good and conscientious work, but would appreciate being reimbursed for the motel bill. I will look forward to hearing from you.

Sincerely,

These three letters are based on complaints I've heard people make. Whether the actual complainers ever wrote letters or not I don't know, but I think these would probably get results. This is what they have going for them:

———

1. The opening sentence sets a reasonable tone rather than going in with guns blasting.

2. The details of complaint are stated clearly but not in an accusatory way. Recipient can tell he isn't dealing with an angry nut case.

3. A touch of flattery is slipped in but also (subtly) the idea that you could be a future enemy instead of a satisfied customer.

4. A clear solution to the problem is offered.

job application cover letters

Whether you have a job now or are just graduating from college, a cover letter not more than three paragraphs long should accompany your résumé. Say briefly who you are, what your present job is and what you would like to be considered for. If you don't know the specific job you want, at least try to be specific about the area you'd like to be in—sales, marketing, research, public relations, advertising, customer relations, etc . . . don't make the letter recipient do all the work of figuring out where you might fit in. Do not, on pain of lighted bamboo shoots under your fingernails (or getting your letter tossed into the wastebasket), try to be funny, gimmicky or amusing. You can avoid irritating the recipient by being brief, friendly and straightforward. It doesn't hurt to say *why* you would like to work for this company . . . flattery can help. Even if you'd be willing to work for cashew nuts, don't discuss money and don't send a photograph. Try to address your letter to a specific person; call the company to get the name of a human resources or recruitment officer. This isn't so easy. Toward writing a sample cover letter for this book, I picked the name of a publishing company—Condé Nast—to see what would happen when I asked for the name of a person to send a job application to. From the phone menu, I finally got a live operator who was so maddening and stuffy (and non-forthcoming with a name!), I finally hung up on her. (I couldn't call my own company, also a publishing house, for the same information because the switchboard operators and people in human resources know my voice and would quickly have supplied a name.) Condé Nast is no different from others. When calling cold you may have to *dig* to get the name of a specific person rather than just a department to send a job application letter to, or maybe you'll know somebody already working in the company who can supply a name. The person you address can pass your letter along to whomever he or she likes. In the last paragraph of your cover letter, be sure to say you will telephone for an appointment for an interview or to come in and fill out an application—then be sure to do so.

Name
Address
Phone/fax

Date

Condé Nast, Inc.
350 Madison Avenue
New York, NY 10017

Dear (name of specific person in human resources or other department):

As a senior majoring in marketing and advertising at Northwestern University, I would like to secure a position in either the fashion or advertising departments of *Vogue, Mademoiselle, Brides* or *Glamour* magazines upon my graduation in May 1998. Having had previous experience in both the fashion and publishing industries, I believe I could make a valuable contribution to your company using creative and communication skills garnered through both education and experience.

Since a letter and résumé can convey only a limited sense of a person's qualifications, I would appreciate the opportunity to meet with you in person to explain my interests and qualifications more fully. I will call your office for an appointment.

Thank you for your time and consideration.

Sincerely,

Name
Address
Phone/fax

Date

Neiman Marcus
1618 Main Street
Dallas, Texas 75201

Dear [specific name]:

Hundreds, perhaps thousands, of people would like to work for Neiman Marcus, the preeminent retail store in the country. I hope the attached résumé will be interesting enough to persuade you to let me come in for an interview.

I am currently a buyer in the china department of Dillard's, where I have been for five years, and would like to be considered for a buying job at Neiman Marcus. If there were an opening in the marketing or advertising departments, I would like to be considered for those as well. I will telephone your office for an appointment.

Sincerely,

résumés

Your name, address, phone/fax number and E-mail go at the top of the page. Then list jobs you have held, starting with your present job, in reverse chronological order. Dates of employment usually go on the left, job descriptions on the right. If you aren't working now—were fired or quit—fudge. Just say "1994 to present." In the job description, give details of what each job consisted of, your responsibilities and how you contributed. Use action verbs. Because they are well done, I have borrowed some résumés from the Human Resources Department of the Hearst Corporation with permission from the applicants, who secured jobs with other companies (they sent résumés to more than one place, as you will). These résumés won't resemble your experience but are examples of comprehensive résumés that got the senders an interview, later a job.

Name
Address
Phone/fax
E-mail

Experience   *TV GUIDE,* **New York, New York**
1993–present   **Research Supervisor** (1996–present)
- Develop sales strategies with Sales, Ad Marketing and Research Departments.
- Collaborate on special projects with Publisher, Research Director and Research manager.
- Create local market and national sales presentations.
- Recommend the acquisition of data/software for the Research Department.
- Test and troubleshoot the latest media research software and systems.
- Supervise and train a Junior Analyst on Research methodologies and techniques.

Senior Research Analyst (1995–1996)
- Devised sales strategies using media and marketing data.
- Developed and analyzed reader studies for general and client specific purposes.
- Created and analyzed multimedia reports for the cable and broadcast industries.
- Assessed the trends of the publishing industry in a series of reports for a Vice President under Rupert Murdoch.
- Performed daily searches on the Internet to keep up-to-date on the latest industry news.
- Worked with Corporate Research Director on special projects and presentations.

Research Analyst (1994–1995)
- Designed and produced presentations with ad sales and marketing departments.
- Developed companywide research reports and competitive sales scenarios.
- Generated and analyzed syndicated and primary data to create sales story.
- Researched new product categories for sales concentration.
- Maintained and updated computer systems and software.

Junior Research Analyst (1993–1994)
- Assisted Senior Analyst in analyzing syndicated data to develop sales strategies.
- Maintained and updated computer systems and software.

1992–1993 **SIMMONS MARKET RESEARCH BUREAU,** New York, New York
Account Representative
- Trained clients on computer systems, coding techniques and data interpretation.
- Daily responsibilities included direct client interaction, troubleshooting, and generation and analysis of Simmons data.

Computer Systems Windows 3.1/95, DOS, Word, Excel, Powerpoint, Harvard Graphics, Lotus 1–2–3, Paradox, Access, IMS, Windsor, New Age, MRI, Simmons, JD Power, Scarborough, CMR, Nielsen America On-line, Netscape, Microsoft Explorer, Dialog

Education B.A. Psychology, 1991, The George Washington University, Washington, D.C.

Awards Helping Hand Award for Research, 1995
Sales Support Person of the Month, June 1996

Name
Address
Phone/fax
E-mail

Experience
1997–Present

EDITOR, **Cliff Street Books,** an imprint of HarperCollins, New York, NY
Edit and publish an average of fifteen books a year in categories from literary fiction to blockbuster self-help, inspiration to thrillers, social commentary to fashion and style; assist the publisher in launching the Cliff Street imprint; develop new writers and support already successful authors; oversee every detail of publication to ensure it is coordinated to that particular project; develop innovative and aggressive marketing plans; write jacket copy, promotional material and marketing sheets for each title; present each title's publishing plan at company sales conferences; prepare profit and loss analyses on prospective acquisitions; negotiate contracts with authors and agents.

1996–1997

ASSOCIATE EDITOR, **HarperCollins,** New York, NY
Acquired popular and literary fiction and non fiction for the Adult Trade Division; established and maintained relationships with authors and literary agents; wrote jacket copy, promotional material and marketing sheets for each title; negotiated contracts with authors and agents.

1995–1996

ASSISTANT EDITOR, **HarperCollins,** New York, NY
Worked directly with the Editor in Chief of the Adult Trade Division in all aspects of the publishing process: managed her office; edited manuscripts; targeted marketing and publicity efforts; oversaw jacket and text production and design; wrote marketing sheets for the sales force, reviews of book proposals and jacket copy.

1994–1995

ASSISTANT EDITOR, **Simon & Schuster,** New York, NY
Edited manuscripts and oversaw projects from inception to finished book for the Illustrated Book Department; prepared production cost estimates with the production department; organized photo shoots for jacket and interior art; resolved contractual discussions with authors, agents and packagers; evaluated submissions.

1993–1994

EDITORIAL ASSISTANT, **Simon & Schuster,** New York, NY
Assisted Senior Editor in handling original and packaged illus-

trated books; managed flow of information and proposals; evaluated submissions.

Education
1990–1994
Summers
1991

Bread Loaf School of English, Middlebury, VT
Master of Arts Degree in English; 4.0 GPA.

Princeton University, Princeton, NJ
Bachelor of Arts Degree in English; graduated *cum laude;*
3.7 GPA

1987

Middlesex School, Concord, MA
Diploma with High Honors; Senior Achievement Award for the highest GPA; The Harvard Book Prize for character, scholastic excellence and achievement in extracurriculars.

Volunteer Services

Fund-raising and special event planning for the Wildlife Conservation Society and the Grosvenor Neighborhood House. Class agent for Middlesex School responsible for alumni fund-raising and reunion planning.

Skills and Interests

Microsoft Word, WordPerfect, Lotus 1–2–3, Excel . . . Proficient in French . . . Interested in gardening, cooking, travel, sea-kayaking and fly-fishing.

Name
Address
Phone/fax
E-mail

Career Focus

Professional writing, editing and analysis in a challenging and progressive organization where literary research, critical analysis and oral and written communication skills can be deployed on team focused and self-initiated projects.

Professional Experience

Beacon Press, Boston, MA   07/97–Present
Editorial Assistant

Assist Editor in Chief in all editorial and administrative aspects of trade book
production. Read and evaluate submissions, maintain contact with authors and
literary agents. Compose editorial letters suggesting revisions to authors already
under contract, line-edit manuscripts, oversee production of new titles. Attend
editorial meetings, contribute ideas for new books. Provide administrative
support.

Boston Magazine, Boston, MA   09/96–07/97
Events Editor

Selected events, composed text, chose and acquired related art and oversaw
production of monthly listings of art, music, theater and cultural events in and
around Boston, striving for a more eclectic offering of activities presented in a
readable and appealing format. Monitored the Boston scene, seeking out unique
or late-breaking events. Wrote, assigned spotlight features. Participated in editorial planning and reviews.

Candlewick Press, Cambridge, MA   09/96–12/96
Intern to Special Sales Manager

Conducted market research. Contacted prospective clients, organized and
produced correspondence and mailings. Sought endorsements from environ-
mental organizations for related anthology. Coordinated a targeted promotional
mailing for adolescent health title. Reviewed and categorized all current titles in
order to revise and expand Candlewick's Curriculum Guide. Prepared guide for
use as a sales tool targeting teachers and librarians.

Houghton Mifflin, Boston, MA   07/97–09/96
Editorial Assistant — School Division

Provided administrative and clerical support for Kindergarten Reading Team
producing a bilingual kindergarten reading series. Proofread copy and tracked
galleys. Created the text for curriculum charts and lesson-planning guides.

Widener Library, Harvard University, Cambridge, MA   09/92–06/96
Staff Assistant
  Received and processed research requests for reproduction of various library materials from universities throughout the U.S. and abroad, as well as the local University community and the general public.

Education

Harvard University, Cambridge, MA
B.A., English and American Literature and Language, cum laude, 1996
- Major interests: twentieth-century American novel and poetry; music/jazz in literature.
- Senior Thesis: a new approach to examining narrative prose based on jazz forms and aesthetics in the writings of Rudolph Fisher, Jean Toomer and Toni Morrison.

Activities:
- *Lighthouse* (quarterly publication addressing gender-related issues of interest to college-age women): Editorial Staff Member: item selection; writing; editing; events calendar; production assistance.
- *Radcliffe Choral Society:* three-year participant; Secretary to Executive Committee
- *CHANCE Tutoring Program and Writing Workshop* for disadvantaged youth.

Related Proficiencies & Interests

Facility with library research systems, on-line and Web research. Computer literate (MacIntosh and PC). Critical literary analysis and editing. Piano and voice performance (current member of Oratorio Society of New York). Researching early twentieth-century immigrants with a focus on family experiences for a fictionalized narrative.

Name
Address
Phone/fax
E-mail

Education: **New York University**   New York, NY
Wagner Graduate School of Public Service
Master of Arts Degree in Public Administration, May 1997
- Awarded the Wagner Graduate School of Public Service Dean's Scholarship
- Coursework specializing in the analysis of domestic and international Public Policy
- Capstone entitled "Extended Producer Responsibility and the Automobile Industry"

Rutgers University   New Brunswick, NJ
Bachelor of Arts Degree in History and Political Science, May 1995
- Won the Rutgers University Presidential Scholarship
- Inducted into the Phi Beta Kappa Honor Society
- Junior Year Abroad at Exeter University in Exeter, England, 1993–1994

Professional Experience: **Metropolitan Transportation Authority**   New York, NY
Audit Intern for the Inspector General's Office, March 1996–May 1997
- Key member of task force that investigated property acquisition and monitoring of labor charges at New York City Transit
- Synthesized interviews, reports, in-house and external memoranda
- Compiled and analyzed data, and created charts and graphs

New York City Parks and Recreation   New York, NY
Intern for Commissioner Henry J. Stern, January–May 1997
- Drafted and edited letters answering the concerns of constituents and government officials
- Performed general office work, including answering phones, fact-checking and word processing

Riker, Danzig, Scherer, Hyland, and Peretti Morristown, NJ
Legal Assistant, June–August 1995
- Assisted with trial preparations, depositions and closings

- Inspected documents for production, and organized documents into efficient filing systems

Senator Bill Bradley   Newark, NJ
Public History Intern, January–May 1995
- Orally communicated and advised on diverse constituent concerns
- Shaped and visualized plans for the Senator's in-state appearances

Congressman Dean Gallo   Washington, DC
Legislative Intern, June–August 1992
- Updated the Congressman on the status of bills on the House floor
- Wrote letters to constituents regarding substantive policy issues

Skills:
- Proficient in WordPerfect, Microsoft Word, Windows, Lotus 123, Excel, Quattro Pro, SPSS and the Internet
- Excellent written and oral communication skills
- Strong research and analytical ability

fan letters

Nobody, from the biggest star to a local school board official, doesn't appreciate hearing about his or her wonderfulness. You may not get a personal response, though you *are* apt to get *something*. Major and lesser movie stars often have fan clubs that handle mail and will even send a signed (photocopy) photograph on request . . . possibly not what you had in mind. Barbara Walters, a gracious and thoughtful celebrity, responds to mail from people she doesn't know with one of several already-created letters, personalized for a particular correspondent. Many celebrities do this. Andy Rooney says, "The letters I get from people who like what I said are better-spelled than the letters from people who are never to going to watch *60 Minutes* again!" Andy answers some of his mail personally, the rest goes to Audience Service, which answers or at least acknowledges letters for him. Years before we became friends, Art Buchwald sent a postcard in response to an out-of-control fan letter from me: "Dear Helen, you made my day and my days aren't easy to make. Sincerely, Art." I thought the message darling and just for me . . . now I know that same card has gone to thousands.

As for getting to be friends with a celebrity through correspondence, if you keep sending letters of appreciation and praise to somebody not *really* famous and don't send them weekly and don't want anything, you may get to be writing friends. Leslie Dart, vice president of P.M.K. Public Relations, which handles publicity for some of the biggest stars in entertainment, tells me Mariah Carey's music company recently hired as a receptionist someone who had written Mariah endlessly and really seemed to understand her idol's music and message. Sylvester Stallone eventually married a young woman— Brigitte Nielsen—after she sent photographs and a letter up to his hotel room, waited in the lobby and he sent for her. Doesn't always turn out that way.

I don't think I ever *didn't* respond to a fan letter, usually *not* with a form letter unless somebody was asking for money, but I'm not a huge celebrity receiving a daily avalanche of mail, plus I love writing letters—not everybody does. When Elizabeth Taylor let me interview her for a profile in *Cosmo* a few years ago and had been wonderful—article turned out well—I sent a letter and an antique brooch. No response. The brooch wasn't in the Richard Burton one hundred-carat Cartier diamond category, but I'd have been happy to keep it for myself. You always wonder if people *got* what you sent, but this went to her house and I think she did. Frank Sinatra didn't write a personal letter when I sent a kind of priceless collection of lyrics of every popular song recorded between 1933 and 1945, painstakingly transcribed from the radio in shorthand by my sister Mary after she got polio, later typed in a songbook . . . hundreds of lyrics. I felt the lyrics could have jogged the memory of a singer wanting to pull in songs from those years. Someone in Frank's office wrote . . . better than not hearing, I guess. I had better luck with the president of the United States, as I mentioned earlier.

Anyway, from receiving some and writing a *ton* of fan letters, here are some pointers, if I may:

1. Most of the pleasure of writing fan letters has to be in the writing—you are moved to get something out of your soul in a well-constructed little letter. Creating a friendship by mail can't be planned on, though it could happen.

2. Type or word-process if you can. If writing by hand, keep penmanship neat, lots of space between the lines. On pain of Chinese water torture, do not write on both sides of the paper unless it's bond.

3. Resist telling your idol the story of your life. He or she won't be riveted and may not even read it. You can get into the act a little by explaining what in your background makes this person so meaningful to you, but basically the letter is to praise his or her writing, speaking, acting, singing, dancing . . . a letter of love and appreciation, not a vehicle for you to unload cares, hopes, ambitions. Advice about life or work from the admired one, I'm afraid you'll have to receive somewhere else.

4. Be specific about what you liked. Quote a few lines in your letter from the play, book or article that impressed you . . . I do that all the time. Repeat lines from his or her performance. "When you said, 'Sorry, Mr. Ambassador, I can't get the peaches into my luggage,' the whole house came down." Report audience reaction. "Two women next to me didn't quiet down for ten minutes after you kissed Matt Damon in the subway." "You could feel tension all over the theater . . . everybody desperately wanted you to get out of that cul-de-sac . . . I think it's called acting!" etc., etc. You can also play back words or thoughts from a television guest's appearance . . . "When you told Sam Donaldson he was too big a person to attack the looks of the attorney general of the United States, I thought that was wonderful!"

Praise, praise, praise . . . approval, approbation . . . nobody gets too much, particularly performers or writers who put themselves on the line.

Words that might go into a fan letter:
"I've just finished reading [book]. Where do I go for pleasure *now*?! Can you write something else fast?"

"[Book] is on my nighttable . . . I finished last night. I'm starting to read all over again."

"Some friends and I discussed your column in *The Washington Post* for an hour yesterday. In a world where lots of people don't seem to get it, you *get* it."

"You were certifiably incredible in [last movie, play]. Now you're back, with *more* incredible! Actors are supposed to be insecure. In your case you could forget 'insecure' the rest of your life."

One of my favorites: "I'm not your mommy but I'm proud of you!"

Do write!

love letters

There should be *more* love letters—unless you're a billionaire bachelor prey to palimony suits by graspy girls to whom you once foolishly put it in writing, or a married politician who enclosed mash notes *with* the red roses and now you, girlfriend and letters are on page 6 of the *New*

York Post. Love letters and sweet notes don't have to be written just to the person you married or plan to, though those recipients may get the tiger's share; love notes can accompany prezzies and flowers to other fortunates.

With a Cannon Elph to current beau: "Angelpie, you are the best-looking male person in the universe, so of course you will not be allowed to keep this camera unless you promise to get pictures taken of *you.* All my love, Gretchen."

The morning after love-making, accompanying masses of daisies to her office: "Ellen, last night was the best night of my life. I'm thirty-four already . . . where *were* you?! I'll call after your meeting . . . Love and hugs, Peter." (I'm big on "hugs" in the sign-off whether the letter is to a lover or a close friend . . . a friendly and innocent word.)

Warning—sorry there has to be one: No passionate or even mildly intense letters to someone who doesn't love you as much as you love him or her, okay? Worms, garter snakes and wet cement are clogging your insides, you ache, long, quiver to pour it all out, hoping to win his or her attention with your love-soaked missive. Are you cuckoo? Such a letter could set *back* the cause, as the recipient perceives deep insecurity there. Writing sweet, friendly letters, particularly to someone away on a trip, is fine. Special time to write: when he or she is going off without you. I often tuck a letter into David's overcoat pocket, shaving kit, or briefcase, to be found when he's unpacking or reading on the plane. "Basker [nickname], I'm so proud of you. You shouldn't be out in the trenches doing what you're doing at your age, I know that, and you hate to leave home so often . . . I feel I'm sending a baby boy into battle but you are a good soldier and will come back with new glory heaped on your beautiful shoulders. Go for a swim every day . . . you *know* that swimming is the enemy of tortilla soup. Don't have more than one scotch and half a bottle of wine at any one meal. Stay out of the Bel Air bar with anything female unless she's on my approved list—very short list. All my love and come back fast as you can." A letter can surely be tucked into *her* briefcase.

What should a "regular" love letter contain? What you *feel*—plus any other subject matter you like: building the new house, what you did last summer, golden days of your first meeting. It's always good to credit a beloved with magical powers as in "you changed my life." "Astrid, I don't know whether you've noticed but I'm different since you got here. According to my mother and Aunt Sophie, I was perfect already, but you've got me doing stuff I didn't know I could . . . that speech before six hundred computer salesmen in Colorado Springs, starting a kids' soccer team, and maybe your finest achievement . . . you lightened me up . . . I was a stiff. You also lightened my middle—15 pounds off the old midsection so I'll last longer which I want to do if you promise to last *with* me. I want to be here forever if you promise to be here forever too. Love and adoration, Seth." Or simpler, "Astrid, you've improved me, been patient with me, loved me into being somebody different and I think better than I was. Do you feel the power? You have it . . . over *me*! All my love, Seth."

To a man or woman on no particular occasion: "Dearest . . . your love . . . caring, being there . . . in bed, yes—I'm besotted with you—but straight up as well, reassure me this is the right lifetime to have been born in because it's the one *you're* in. I just wanted to tell you that before I plopped off to sleep. [Angus, Lydia]"

Need to apologize? "Dearest, was I a little out of control last night (and what do I mean 'a little'?). I'm so very sorry. I know I've got to do something about my temper and saying I'd had a bad day doesn't excuse anything. Please be home by 7:00 tonight if you can. We'll open the Taitinger '87 and I'll toast your being the best [wife, husband] there is and me the luckiest [man/woman] alive. I love you with all my heart. [Spencer, Paula]."

Woman to husband or lover: "Murray, did I tell you recently I've not only got you under my skin, deep in the heart of me (thank you, Cole Porter), I've got you in my *brain*. All day long funny things you've said, tender things, smart things keep coming back [quote a couple of these if you can]. When I consider the other women you could have married [could be with], and we both know who they are, I am still wondrous and joyful that you picked *me*. I know you don't like mushy but consider this a special curse . . . a wife [girlfriend] who can't quit saying how wonderful you are and how much she loves you. Jennifer."

And one of my favorites: "Dear Karen, you know how some doggies can't pass a telephone pole or fire hydrant without sniffing? Well, I find it almost impossible to get by an outdoor telephone without calling you; I can resist cell phones or calling from the office with people around, but outdoors is a challenge. Just like telephone poles and fire hydrants tell doggies what to do, a street phone gives me this almost primordial urge to call you and hear your voice. Hope you don't get terminally bored . . . just call me Wuffums. All my love . . . Wuffums."

condolence letters

They are important, difficult to write and *must* be sent. These are points you might want to make:

Stress what the bereaved meant to the departed. "[Beloved person's name] adored you. You were a wonderful [wife/husband]."

"Your stamina, love, courage during [his/her] illness was awesome. We watched you, hurt for you, told each other we'd like to be as courageous and caring as you under these circumstances though [name] deserved all that love."

"I never heard any but wonderful things said about

[wife/husband/son]. He/she made all our lives better, left us much too soon."

"My fondest memories of [him/her] are [recount things you did together]."

"Your life will somehow go on and I want to be part of it. I'll look forward to seeing you *soon*" (important to tell widows who assume, not unreasonably, they won't be sought after much with Fred gone).

Add a few words about the funeral or memorial service you thought well done.

And what about this touching letter any of us might be in a position to write someday, though we'll hope not, sent by the author of *Tales of the South Pacific* and many other great books to scores of his friends shortly before he died.

James A. Michener
Austin, Texas

9 October 1997

Dear friends,

It is with a real sadness that I send you what looks to be a final correspondence between us. The medicos have left little doubt that this present illness is terminal. I approach this sad news with regret, but not with any panic. I am surrounded by friends who support in these final moments with the same high spirit they have displayed in the past. And if anyone can keep a man's spirits elated, Debbie and Susan and John and Amelia can certainly do that. I am thus constantly fortified by young people of good spirits, who keep mine high.

I reach the end of my life with almost daily phone calls with beloved friends. Their spirits keep me alert and their reminiscences keep me alive. A constant hum of phone calls keeps me in touch with friends, who bring me joy and a sense of continuing life.

I wish I could visit with each of you, but that would be impossible. The phone calls, however, recall the high-lights of an exciting life. And they cascade back now to remind of the highlights: the running for political office, and the drubbings we took there, the victories we had in the theaters. I savor every memory as they parade past. What a full life they made. And what a joy they bring me now, what a joy your recollection of them gives me now. It is in this mood that my final days are being passed. And I thank you all for your thoughtfulness.

Fondly,

James A. Michener

Okay, while others are clamoring for you to *telephone* a loved one you might not have contacted recently, I'm suggesting *write*. Off to the note sheets or word-processor with you!

And so it's bye-bye for now. I've had a wonderful time visiting with you and putting this book together. If it ever does *anything* to help you into print, I hope you'll write and tell me about it. The important thing is to start *writing . . . now*. You're a writer!